IMAGES
of America

McClellanville
and the St. James,
Santee Parish

A historical marker on Highway 17 at McClellanville's north entrance explains its formative history. The marker's text continues on the reverse side: " . . . cotton, naval stores and seafoods. Incorporated in 1926 and encircled by the Francis Marion National Forest and Cape Romain National Wildlife Refuge, McClellanville is best known for its shrimp fleet and seafood industries. Except for a period during the Civil War, two lighthouses in the Wildlife Refuge served as beacons to coastal shipping from 1827 to 1947." The marker was erected in 1995 by the St. James Santee Historical Society, founded in 1981. This section of Highway 17 is named for James Mitchell Graham, a native son of McClellanville who chaired Charleston County Council from 1957 to 1964.

ON THE COVER: A view of the Wedge Plantation, built about 1826 on the South Santee River, typifies parish life a century ago. Worn buildings and late-19th-century clothing styles contrast with the latest transportation, the automobile. Framing this vignette is a Lowcountry icon, the moss-draped live oak tree. The Wedge survived other plantations lost to neglect or fire and was sold by Dr. Richard B. Dominick's estate to the University of South Carolina in 1976. (Courtesy of South Carolina Historical Society.)

IMAGES
of America

McClellanville
and the St. James,
Santee Parish

Susan Hoffer McMillan and
Selden Baker "Bud" Hill

ARCADIA
PUBLISHING

Published by Arcadia Publishing
Charleston, South Carolina

Library of Congress Catalog Card Number: 2006920410

For all general information contact Arcadia Publishing at:
Telephone 843-853-2070
Fax 843-853-0044
E-mail sales@arcadiapublishing.com
For customer service and orders:
Toll-Free 1-888-313-2665

Visit us on the Internet at www.arcadiapublishing.com

*This book is dedicated to the many individuals, living and deceased,
who collected and recorded the history of
McClellanville and St. James, Santee Parish to be treasured forever.*

CONTENTS

Acknowledgments   6

Introduction   7

1.   McClellanville   11

2.   Parish Plantations and Churches   79

3.   Other Landmarks   109

ACKNOWLEDGMENTS

The authors appreciate all who helped make this book possible. Many of its images are from the Sylvan Racine Collection of the Village Museum in McClellanville. These and others were supplied by the generous families of the village and the surrounding area. Accompanying historical texts were derived from oral interviews and from David Doar's 1907 address, "A Sketch of the Agricultural Society of St. James Santee, South Carolina," and an address on the traditions and reminiscences of the parish, documenting the area's rich past. Additional historical information was gleaned from such publications as *St. James Santee Plantation Parish History and Records, 1685–1925* by Anne Baker Leland Bridges and Roy Williams III; *St. James Santee Parish Historical Sketches*, edited by Bennett Baxley; *The Visible Village, McClellanville 1860–1945* by William P. Baldwin; and *Home in the Village* by Walter Bonner. Publisher Lauren Bobier of Arcadia Publishing and editors Adam Ferrell and Adam Latham enthusiastically supported this book, and their encouragement and assistance was most helpful.

Special appreciation is extended to Mary Barry, Dr. Nic Butler and Lish Thompson of Charleston County Public Library, James Carolina of Georgetown County Public Library, Mary Catherine Cecil, Mike Coker and John Tucker of South Carolina Historical Society, Dr. Jonathan Lucas Dieter, Lillian Duke, Wes Dunson, Mary Lucas Easley, Judy Stroman Fortner, Bobby Graham, Connie Graham, Frances Graham, Lyda Graham, Jim Grayson, Pat Gross of McClellanville Library, Thomasine Graham Harvin, Debbie Thames Hattaway, Joel Jackson, Margy Graham Leland, Stuart Mackintosh, Jimmy McClellan, Gene Morrison, Ethel Trenholm Seabrook Nepveux, Ginny and Michael Prevost, Sylvan Racine, Dr. Frank Sanders, Sarah Nell Scott, Terry Read Scott, Debbie Summey of Georgetown County Museum, Julie Warren of Hampton Plantation, Sally Warren, Dean Woerner, and Martha Zierden.

The authors hope this volume encourages the rediscovery and dissemination of forgotten images in archival family sources. Gratitude is extended to family and friends who provided understanding and support while we compiled the book, especially to Marshall.

INTRODUCTION

"Nowhere else in the world has nature been kinder to her children than in those regions where the great plantations were formed out of the Eden-like wilderness of the Low Country. And that charm is an eternal one; though the civilization that it cradled and nourished has passed away, the charm survives." These are the words that native son and poet Archibald Hamilton Rutledge used to describe the region once known as St. James, Santee Parish. To understand the history of the little village called McClellanville, it's necessary to take a retrospective look at the parish.

The vast wilderness known as St. James, Santee Parish, stretching along the coast of the Carolina Colony from Awendaw Creek to the mouth of the great Santee Rivers, was incorporated into the Church of England in 1706 and was the first parish organized outside of Charles Town. At the time of its founding, the boundary lines of the parish extended from the Atlantic Ocean at the entrances of these two waterways deep inland into the uncharted Carolina wilderness.

The area, however, had long been the home and hunting grounds of the Seewee and Santee tribes; the Seewee tribe established villages along the coast, while the Santee tribe settled farther inland along the banks of the Santee River. Jeremy Creek, on which the village of McClellanville would later be established, was the site of an earlier Seewee village, and the creek itself takes its name from one of the chiefs of the tribe, "King Jeremy."

As early as 1685, the region was inhabited by French Huguenots, the first of that body of immigrants to settle in the Carolina Colony. The Huguenots established plantations, a church, and a small village along the banks of the Santee River at a place they called James Town. John Lawson, the English traveler and early visitor to the area called "French Santee," described the French inhabitants as "a temperate, industrious people, some of them bringing very little effects, yet by their endeavors and mutual assistance amongst themselves, have outstripped our English, who brought with them larger fortunes." At the time of incorporation, there were 100 French and 60 English families already in the area. The settlement of James Town did not prove to be successful, and many of the families chose to settle downriver in the tidewater region.

The plantations of St. James Santee were richly endowed. These early settlers and their descendants engaged in the culture of indigo, rice, and cotton, and worked in the naval stores industry, making tar, rosin, and turpentine for the building of ships. Indigo leaves, from which a blue dye was derived, was the first crop to promise great wealth, and it continued to do so until the colonies became independent of England, the main customer for the product. The crop was abandoned sometime between 1790 and 1794, when England withdrew the American bounty on indigo and brought the products of her other colonies into competition. The growing of rice in the parish overlapped and eventually replaced indigo. Planters learned through experience that rice, first grown on high land, would grow better in the damp spots and in inland swamps, so low land along creeks and the edge of the river was cleared, including the lands of the fertile Santee Delta. The importation of slaves from African regions with a history of rice cultivation, the development of a system for flooding and draining fields, and the invention by Jonathan Lucas of a water-driven rice mill for removing the hull from the grain all came together in the

7

late 1700s and made the planters of St. James Santee leaders in the production of the high quality rice known as Carolina Gold.

By 1735, when rice cultivation was at its zenith, homes of great architectural grandeur were built, two of which stand today, Fairfield and Hampton, attesting to the prosperity of the parish. In 1768, the third church of St. James Santee was built. It was situated in a vast forest once called "the Ocean" and stands along the road that led from Charleston to Virginia, known as the Old Kings Highway. It was there that men of national distinction worshipped, many of whom it is said helped establish a lasting foundation for the new republic and for the state of South Carolina.

Rice followed cotton as the region's major cash crop, even though most of the land was very low. St. James Santee continued to prosper and to influence the economic, political, and cultural development of the nation and state until the Civil War. Planters of the region struggled with planting both rice and cotton well into the early 1900s, but the times had changed. The erosion of planters' great wealth, the emancipation and scattering of their work force, and competition from other states all brought their glory days to an end. Many turned back to the woods for income. Men from Horry County, South Carolina, and Brunswick County, North Carolina, came and reestablished the naval stores industry.

Shortly before the Civil War, summer resorts, "as much for social purpose as for health," according to planter David Doar, were established by the planters of the region at the mouth of the Santee River on Murphy's and Cedar Islands. The community of Honey Hill and one at the end of Seven Mile Road sprang up. All except Honey Hill would eventually combine at a site on the banks of a picturesque tidal tributary called Jeremy Creek. The place remained nameless for years, until it was finally agreed that the name should be McClellanville after one of the founding fathers.

The two adjoining parcels of land, Point Plantation and Jeremy Plantation, on which the village was built, were owned by Archibald James McClellan and Richard Tillia Morrison II, who sold or leased lots to a few planters—men with well-established family names such as Cordes, Leland, Whilden, Pinckney, Manigault, Doar, and DuPre. Reddin Baxley, the postmaster at Santee, and Dr. Edward Darrell Smith, the local physician, also bought lots. McClellan's homestead at Point Plantation was situated in the heart of the new village. Morrison, whose main residence was at Laurel Hill Plantation, just south of the village, also built a summerhouse. Today the boundary line between the two original tracts is Oak Street.

A schoolhouse was completed in 1858. William Peter Beckman built the first store after the Civil War, and more homes were erected over time. Many homes built in the 1890s reflect designs influenced by the Victorian period.

Around 1898, some of the old rice plantations of the parish were purchased and combined into hunting preserves to be enjoyed by wealthy sportsmen, primarily from the North. The Santee Club, the Kinloch Club, the Cape Romain Club, and other duck-hunting clubs were established. Pres. Grover Cleveland was a frequent visitor and hunter, as were some of the nation's great industrialists, lawyers, bankers, railroad men, and former generals.

Eventually McClellanville took on the look of a real town, with several churches and a main street lined with busy shops. Local folks and people from nearby towns and farms shopped at McClellanville, mainly on Saturdays. There was an ice cream parlor, a butcher shop, three pharmacies (some with soda fountains), five or six general merchandise stores selling everything from groceries and hardware to clothing and caskets, several barber shops, the Bank of McClellanville, and a post office. Later there was a shop that sold furniture and RCA Victor talking machines, as well as one dealing in fine hats for ladies. Many different businesses have come and gone, including canning companies that packed and shipped crabmeat, oysters, tomatoes, okra, and other products.

In the late 1920s, when a bridge spanning the Cooper River and leading into Charleston was built, the coastal highway (now Highway 17) was paved, and bridges crossing the rivers leading to Georgetown were completed, villagers traveled to the big cities to shop. Their new automobiles, the new highway, and the new bridges made the trip much easier and almost comfortable. The shops of the village suffered greatly, and many closed their doors forever.

In the 1930s and 1940s, a seafood industry sprang up; it was centered on the harvesting of shrimp, oysters, clams, and crabs. Over time, this new industry replaced timbering and truck farming as the main source of income for the people of the village. McClellanville is now known as one of South Carolina's most picturesque and productive fishing villages. Its economy is now largely dependent upon the sea rather than the land. Today the village is surrounded, and somewhat protected, by the Francis Marion National Forest and by the Cape Romain National Wildlife Refuge.

The images in this book focus on the architectural and cultural history of the town of McClellanville and that of the parish that preceded it. Images chosen for this book depict the extraordinary way of life in the "old rice parish" and show the easygoing everyday life of the village. They also tell the story of a region that one celebrated writer termed "the most humane and the most chivalric civilization that America has ever known" and that of the village that grew from it.

A McClellanville Blessing

Bless our Village home, oh Lord, we cry.
Please keep it cool in mid-July.

Bless the walls where termites dine,
While ants and roaches march in time.

Bless our yard where spiders pass
Fire ant castles in the grass.

Bless the garage, a home to please
Carpenter beetles, ticks and fleas.

Bless the love bugs, two by two,
The gnats and mosquitoes that feed on you.

Millions of creatures that fly and crawl,
In our Village, Lord, you've put them all!!!

But this is home, and here we'll stay,
So thank you Lord, for insect spray.

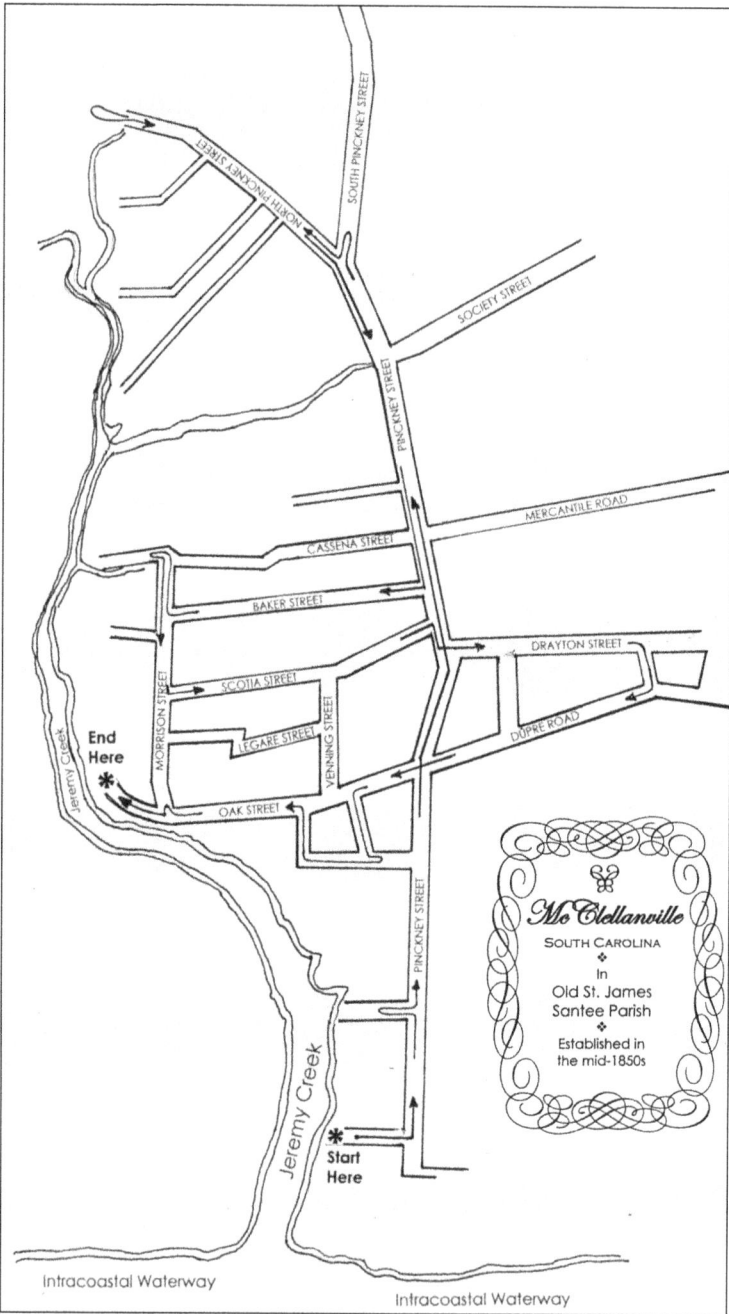

Map labels (as drawn):

- SOUTH PINCKNEY STREET
- NORTH PINCKNEY STREET
- SOCIETY STREET
- PINCKNEY STREET
- MERCANTILE ROAD
- CASSENA STREET
- BAKER STREET
- DRAYTON STREET
- MORRISON STREET
- SCOTIA STREET
- LEGARE STREET
- VENNING STREET
- DUPRE ROAD
- Jeremy Creek
- **End Here** ✳
- OAK STREET
- PINCKNEY STREET
- ✳ **Start Here**
- *Mc Clellanville*
- SOUTH CAROLINA
- ❖
- In
- Old St. James
- Santee Parish
- ❖
- Established in
- the mid-1850s
- Intracoastal Waterway
- Intracoastal Waterway

A village map drawn by Bud Hill suggests a route through McClellanville's historic district beginning at Jeremy Creek near the terminus of Pinckney Street and returning to the creek beside the shrimp boat wharfs at the terminus of Oak Street. The route follows the book's sequence, offering views of most historic-district village properties identified as pre-1940 construction and explained herein by accompanying histories. Inclusion of noteworthy citizens, village-life scenes, and additional properties affords readers a broader village history. Turn arrows on the map are directional changes conforming to the geographical placement of buildings and people so that readers may use the book for a self-guided, walking village tour.

One

McClellanville

Henrietta Baker Hill, right, and her unidentified friends pose beside Jeremy Creek a century ago. Hill was the village's first Charleston Free Library librarian and first school librarian. She was also the grandmother of this book's coauthor, Bud Hill. Nearby is the Robert E. Ashley Boat Landing, named for a former village mayor, and the Lowcountry Seaman's Memorial, a granite marker listing persons drowned at sea.

A bird's-eye village view, c. 1935, was seen from the fire lookout tower near the mouth of Jeremy Creek. The town developed around 1858 when its two forefathers subdivided their plantations and sold lots. Archibald James McClellan's Point Plantation comprised most property east of Oak Street. Richard Tillia Morrison II of Laurel Hill Plantation owned Jeremy Plantation, comprising most property west of Oak Street.

McClellanville's fire lookout tower was built about 1935 to support the adjacent U.S. Biological Survey office that managed Cape Romain Migratory Bird Refuge, now Cape Romain National Wildlife Refuge. First used as a bird observatory, this rusting sentinel has witnessed decades of village dependency on seafood industries and a recent renewal of tourism, which is what started McClellanville.

A coastal view from the fire lookout tower shows the Intracoastal Waterway and marsh islands beyond it, buffering McClellanville from the sea. A concrete block building with a Spanish-tile roof (foreground) opened in 1935 as a U.S. Biological Survey office, later renamed the wildlife refuge headquarters. The $60,000 office building originally included three bedrooms, a four-car garage, a boat house, and a wharf.

South Carolina Crab Company was on Jeremy Creek near the Intracoastal Waterway from its beginning as Maryland Crab Company in 1963 until it closed in 2002. It was replaced with residential development. Here locally harvested Atlantic blue crabs were hand-picked by African Americans. Once operating as Thomas Seafood, the crab company's 20-plus workers processed 400 to 500 pounds of crabmeat daily.

The Richard Morrison Lofton house, built about 1892 at 314 Lofton Court, was named Around the Beach. Destroyed in 1989 by Hurricane Hugo, the house had experienced changes and additions over time, much like its land, which grew to be a family farm. Lofton married Lillian Edith Stroman, and they had nine children. Several grandchildren live in modern homes built on this old family homestead.

The former wildlife refuge headquarters, which was built to facilitate migratory bird studies, is pictured here in 1945. The 401 Pinckney Street building housed various businesses, as well as town hall, before the Village Museum opened here in April 1999. Village and parish history combine with marine culture in this 2,000-square-foot interpretative facility. This is the former site of a historic home (explained on page 45). The wildlife refuge headquarters is now at 5821 Highway 17 in Awendaw.

John Hugh Graham's house, built around 1914 at 408 Pinckney Street, had a carbide-light plant behind this property, now on the National Register of Historic Places. Graham owned a village hardware and furniture store in his name and was an attorney and an area distributor for Standard Oil of New Jersey. Beginning with Graham, three generations of his family served in the state legislature. He married Marie Mitchell of Saluda, who is holding one of their four children, Thomasine Graham. (Courtesy of Thomasine Graham Harvin.)

Dr. John Young DuPre had his grandfather's c. 1790 home disassembled and floated by barge from Echaw Plantation, South Santee River, to McClellanville in 1861. It was rebuilt on a $200 lot at 423 Pinckney Street as a summer home for DuPre and his wife, Mary Rebecca Jerman, of Ashton Plantation near Jamestown. She soon died, and DuPre sold the house in 1869 for $1,000 to his brother, Andrew Hibben DuPre, who married Esther A. McClellan.

Dr. John Y. DuPre (1827–1900) sits beside his brother, James Hamlin DuPre, around 1860. DuPre pioneered the influx of wealthy planter families with summer retreats in McClellanville, beginning shortly before his Civil War service. Afterward he practiced medicine for 50 years in nearby Christ Church Parish. The Huguenot-influenced DuPre house is the village's oldest residence and is on the National Register of Historic Places.

The Lillian Farmer Lucas house at 431 Pinckney Street was built after Lucas purchased her lot from Dr. John Y. DuPre for $600 in 1925. A native of Florence, South Carolina, Lucas taught elementary school in the village for 38 years, retired in 1959, and died in 1971. She married Alexander Hume Lucas Jr., a planter.

Design of the Huguenot-style Archibald Hamilton Seabrook house, 211 Rutledge Court, is credited to Alexander H. Lucas. It was built in 1891 by freed slave carpenter Paul B. Drayton as a summer home for Seabrook and his wife, Caroline C. Pinckney, of El Dorado Plantation on the South Santee River. Seabrook purchased his Jeremy Creek lot from Andrew H. DuPre for $400.

Arthur Stanland McClellan's house, built about 1891 at 208 Rutledge Court, was named Summer Home. McClellan ran a sawmill and lived on Old Kings Highway near Brick Church. His sturdy cottage survived hurricanes in 1893, 1916, and 1989. McClellan's father, Lawrence Perry McClellan, earlier acquired this property from his father, Archibald J. McClellan, and burned oyster shells in a kiln on its point, producing lime.

The Martha A. Taylor house was built about 1882 by Paul B. Drayton. She and her seaman husband, George, had eight children. They included Eliza Taylor Murray, who built next door; Dan Taylor, a boat captain; and Jane Frances Taylor, a teacher of 46 years for whom a local school building was named. The house's lot at 506 Pinckney Street was bought from Archibald J. McClellan in 1875 for $100.

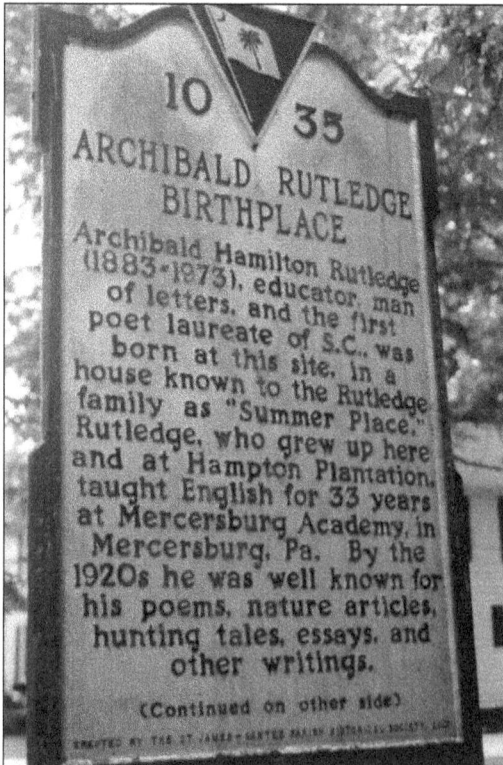

A historical marker recalls the 511 Pinckney Street log-cabin retreat of South Carolina's first poet laureate, Archibald Hamilton Rutledge. It was destroyed by Hurricane Hugo in 1989. Rutledge was born and died in this home, which was built for his parents, Col. and Mrs. Henry Middleton Rutledge, and was named Summer Place. Attorney planter Gabriel Manigault earlier acquired the lot in 1861 from Archibald J. McClellan.

Eliza Ann Taylor Murray's house at 514 Pinckney Street was built soon after her mother conveyed to her in 1914 a lot adjoining her childhood home. Like several village homes, it faces the ocean. Murray married Jasper John Murray, a sailor, and they had three children. They moved to Charleston in 1920, and this became the family home of Dr. Arthur L. Dantzler, a pharmacist at the village's Red Cross Pharmacy.

Willie Joe Tuten's house is a one-and-one-half-story brick-veneer residence at 522 Pinckney Street, built c. 1930. She was a daughter of Roland Hughes and Mary Harriet "Hattie" Graham and was named for her uncles, William Isaiah Graham and Joseph Graham. She married Larry Tuten from Yemassee, and he taught agriculture in the village school. The couple had one surviving child, Mary Margaret Tuten, and they moved to California.

White Gables is a Country Victorian house built in 1897 by Wade Hampton Graham for his first wife, Lilla Hughes. Following her death, Graham married Sarah Jane "Jenny Hamp" Stanland. For decades, Stanland ran her 528 Pinckney Street home as a boarding house. Single school teachers boarding here usually stayed to marry village sons. Graham delivered mail and co-owned Bulls Bay Canning Company with a brother, T. W. Graham Jr. (Courtesy of Charleston County Public Library.)

The James Osgood McClellan Sr. house was built about 1914 at 532 Pinckney Street, opposite his parents' Point Plantation. After his father's premature death, McClellan became the head of household at age 16. He married Louise Augusta Whilden, and they had nine children. McClellan ran a boat, the *Atlas*, and later opened a store, J. O. McClellan, General Merchandise, at 933 South Pinckney Street.

The *Atlas* was a passenger and freight boat traveling between Charleston and McClellanville in the early 20th century. It belonged to John M. Lofton Jr. for most of its existence and was sold to James O. McClellan around 1917. The boat was hit and sank near Charleston some years later without compensation, so McClellan began a new career as a village merchant.

Point Plantation, also called Old Point or McClellan Plantation, is the 490-acre Archibald McClellan Sr. (1740–1791) homestead of 1771. Its name reflects a promontory of land on Jeremy Creek. McClellan emigrated from Perth, Scotland, and his grandson, Archibald James McClellan (1814–1880), was the village's codeveloper. This house, in an oak grove at 533 Pinckney Street, replaced the original pre-Revolutionary home that burned in 1902.

The *Happy Days*, seen in Jeremy Creek, was a 35-foot boat belonging to Santee Gun Club from 1906 to 1925. Built with a gasoline engine, it was converted to a wood-burning, twin-screw steam engine before the gun club received it. The boat traveled eight miles an hour and rode too low for use, except in calm weather. Stripped of a kitchen and sleeping quarters in 1925, *Happy Days* became a village freight and passenger boat. (Courtesy of Lyda Graham.)

James Armstrong Lofton's house was built about 1908 at 546 Pinckney Street. He was lauded as a state legislator in 1946 for having the toll removed on the Cooper River Bridge, which opened in 1929. Lofton married Caroline Juliet Stroman, and they had seven children, including Lt. Col. Juliet Lofton and U.S. Amb. Harry Lofton. A second marriage to Apsley McClellan yielded one additional child. (Courtesy of Charleston County Public Library.)

Robert Edward Graham's house was built about 1915 at 549 Pinckney Street. Graham was a partner with two of his brothers in the general merchandise store T. W. Graham and Company. This home later received a rear addition and a side porch. Graham married Agnes Reynolds Morrison, daughter of Eliza Hibben Leland and James Brown Morrison, and they had three children, in whose family the house remains. (Courtesy of Lyda Graham.)

The Julia R. Lofton King house, 554 Pinckney Street, had the village's first screen porch, referred to by her housekeeper as "the sieve." The house was built about 1898 on a $200 lot acquired from Laura Moore McClellan, widow of John Palmer McClellan. The owner was a daughter of Henry Michael Lofton and Susan Ann Morrison, and she married William Adolph King, who was later mayor of Mount Pleasant.

The Ida Brailsford Whilden house, 555 Pinckney Street, was built about 1903, according to a signature board found during renovation. An annex to the adjacent boarding house, it had a kitchen and bathroom added after it sold in 1943 for $1,000 and was later called Moon Dog Manor. Whilden was a spinster daughter of Elias John Whilden and Selena Morrison Brailsford. She launched the village school lunch program and lived over 100 years.

The Sallie McClellan Fairchild house, built about 1890 at 559 Pinckney Street, is an angular house with an unusual entrance through the dining room, a focal point when Fairchild offered room and board to travelers. She was a daughter of Archibald J. McClellan and Elizabeth J. Steele. She married J. M. Phillips and had a son. Later widowed, she married Confederate veteran Daniel Fairchild of Charleston.

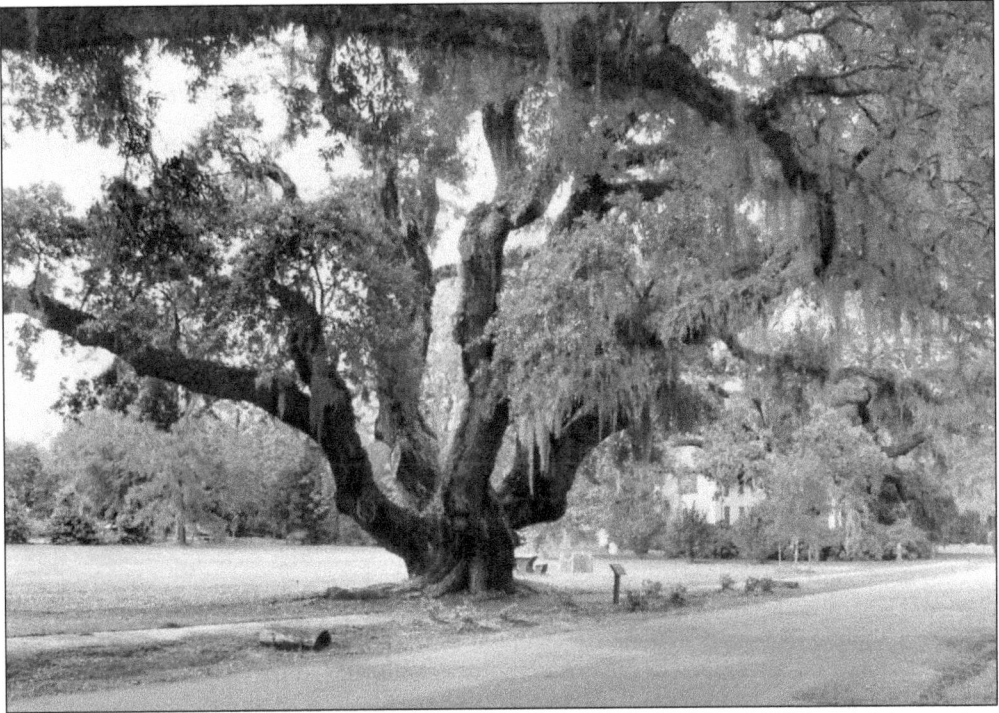

Deerhead Oak Park, at the corner of Pinckney and Oak Streets, celebrates the town's largest live oak tree, which has a 30.6-foot circumference and is estimated to be over 1,000 years old. One of its massive, gnarled branches resembles a deer head with limbs spread like antlers. Before 1868, German immigrant William P. Beckman (1834–1895) owned the village's first retail business, a combined general store and home, beside this tree.

Comparison of a 1946 postcard of McClellanville United Methodist Church, 568 Pinckney Street, with the actual church reveals a steeple modification and a missing chimney. The church was built in 1903 on the former site of Point Plantation's slave village, land given by Elizabeth J. Steele McClellan, the widow of Archibald J. McClellan. Early village plats show six slave cabins on this property.

A Methodist church plaque reads, "On September 21, 1989, Hurricane Hugo, a Category 4 storm, crossed the South Carolina coast at Bulls Bay. Calculated ground wind speed was 138 mph with gusts to 179 mph. The tidal surge in the [church] was 16.25 feet, indicated by the top of this plaque. Damage was extensive. Donations from throughout the United States made restoration possible. We extend our thanks to those who blessed us with their generosity."

The Millard F. Skipper house, 606 Pinckney Street, was built about 1904 by African American carpenter Julius Brown, who constructed a similar house for himself nearby. Skipper's primary home was across Jeremy Creek, where he built Silver Hill Plantation and gave land in 1873 for a village cemetery. The front door, above, was later removed so the house would front Dupre Road. It was once a restaurant called Skipper's Chowder House. (Courtesy of Charleston County Public Library.)

Millard Fillmore Skipper (1854–1920) expanded area production of naval stores that had been introduced locally by his father. A son of John Boswell Skipper and Sarah Eleanor Hilbern, he married Lillian Wiggins without issue. The elder Skipper arrived from eastern North Carolina in 1858 and acquired Palmer's Point Plantation, part of which retains his name as Skipper's Point, across Jeremy Creek from the village.

A granite marker in Memorial Park, at the corner of Pinckney and Oak Streets, honors 131 parish residents who served in World War II. The park was donated in 1859 by Richard T. Morrison II for a combined village church and school facility and donated in 1946 by the Charleston County School District for a park. Henry T. Morrison chaired the marker committee, and Archibald Rutledge spoke at its 1946 unveiling, shown here.

A former village post office, 628 Pinckney Street, is now a residence. The concrete-block and brick-veneer building dispensed mail from 1958 to 1981. Triweekly mail service arrived in McClellanville by 1908, bringing with it the village's first automobile, a chain-driven Oldsmobile Reo. The mailman was seldom alone on trips to Mount Pleasant, as villagers considered his automobile their shuttle service.

Arthur Skipper built the Kate Vincent Waring house, 634 Pinckney Street, before 1904. She married James Cash Waring, who was rector of St. James Santee Episcopal Church from 1898 to 1902, when he resigned the clergy to study medicine. He returned to the village as a physician and had an office on Pinckney Street. Though vacant for many years, the house is now restored. (Courtesy of Charleston County Public Library.)

PRESBYTERIAN CHURCH McCLELLANVILLE S.C.

New Wappetaw Presbyterian Church, 635 Pinckney Street, was built about 1875 on land given by Robert V. Morrison. This is the third sanctuary for the church, which was organized on Seewee Bay in 1696 as Wappetaw Independent Church and was later burned by British troops. Also called Old Wappetaw Church, the early church has a cemetery (shown on page 107). This church's steeple originally sat beside the sanctuary.

Members of the Presbyterian Church Ladies' Aid Society prepare to leave following a meeting in October 1950. They are, from left to right, Belle Morrison, Ouida Leland, Lucille Leland, Minnie Beckman, and Margaret Koelling. Also attending were Jenny Wells, Lou Kirkley, Mae Brailsford, and Louise Stroman. They met for Christian fellowship while quilting to raise church funds.

The Julius Brown house, 704 Pinckney Street, attests to the carpentry skills of African American carpenter and owner Julius Brown. He constructed this house and the nearby Millard F. Skipper house in 1904, using the same floor plan but with porch variations. Recently restored, this house was earlier called the Ester Commander house, named for Brown's daughter, who subsequently owned the house.

Julius Brown (1862–1922) was a local carpenter and barber. He and his wife, Caroline, were the parents of Clifford Brown, Phoebe Ann Brown, Marie Brown, Lucia Brown, and Ester Brown Commander. Brown participated in building numerous village structures, including the St. James Santee Chapel of Ease Episcopal Church. He also trimmed hair for all races in a barber shop on a front corner of his lot.

The Bank of McClellanville, right, recalls the village's economic optimism in the early 1900s. The 710 Pinckney Street bank incorporated in 1912 with Richard M. Lofton as president. It failed in 1925, after which the bank building, which was shared by the post office, and a four-acre parcel were auctioned for $880 in 1936. Investors received a 50-percent liquidation return.

McClellanville Public School, 711 Pinckney Street, was built about 1921. An entrance avenue of tall palmetto trees enhances its neoclassical architecture. This school, shown in the 1930s with added classroom extensions, is now McClellanville Middle School. The Jane F. Taylor Cafetorium, a combined cafeteria and auditorium named for a beloved teacher, opened here in 1959.

Girl Scout Troop No. 1 organized in 1921. Their events included an oyster roast at Cape Romain, camping at Ravenswood Plantation on Bulls Island, a fund-raiser in the Masonic Lodge, camping at El Dorado Plantation, a valentine party for the Boy Scouts, a reception for their mothers, camping in Hampton Plantation's ballroom, a cookout at Skipper's Point, a cookout at Tibwin Plantation, and a weekend at Fairfield Plantation.

The James Brown Morrison Jr. house, 718 Pinckney Street, was built about 1914. This symmetrical cottage on brick piers has a metal roof and clapboard siding. Morrison ran a general store in his name at 852 Pinckney Street and married Lillian Ervin of Darlington. He belonged to the social and agricultural organization that began as an antebellum planters' club, the St. James Santee Agricultural Society.

Samuel Leland Baker, who lived at 228 Baker Street, owned the S. L. Baker Store, 725 Pinckney Street. His major store products were dry goods, shoes, groceries, and meats. The store was later sold and became Paul H. Seabrook's general merchandise store. A smaller commercial building now occupies this downtown location.

A former McClellanville fire station, left, at 727 Pinckney Street, was built in 1981 on the site of an earlier firehouse. It has been rehabilitated as a studio and artist-in-residence housing for the McClellanville Arts Council. Next door, right, at 733 Pinckney Street, McClellanville Telephone Company built a one-story brick office, which now houses the arts council's office and retail galleries.

Dr. William Hantz Felder (1898–1951) was an African American physician who was the only village doctor from 1933 until 1939. He then returned with his family to his native Charleston. Felder's medical office, located at 730 Pinckney Street, was in a building that was later razed. He married Margaret I. Mitchell of Greensboro, North Carolina, and they had two children.

McClellanville Mercantile Company's warehouse, built about 1904 at 804 Pinckney Street, no longer exists. It was owned by two brothers who also owned the King Brothers' General Store, which was built about 1902 on the opposite side of T. W. Graham and Company and also no longer exists. The warehouse, which got a face-lift for a movie set and offered antiques for sale in its final years, was razed in 1994.

T. W. Graham and Company, 810 Pinckney Street, was founded in 1894 and is the oldest village business in continuous operation, having started as a general merchandise store and evolved into a restaurant. Graham's store occupied several downtown locations over time. The current facility, built about 1950, has a yesteryear charm and was filmed for scenes in *Paradise*, the 1991 movie starring Melanie Griffith and Don Johnson.

T. W. Graham and Company operated in a series of buildings, including the King Brothers' General Store, which was built about 1902 at 814 Pinckney Street and later was razed. Before bridges connected McClellanville to other coastal ports in the late 1920s, the village had over 20 retail businesses serving about 500 residents. There are currently a dozen retail businesses serving about 350 residents.

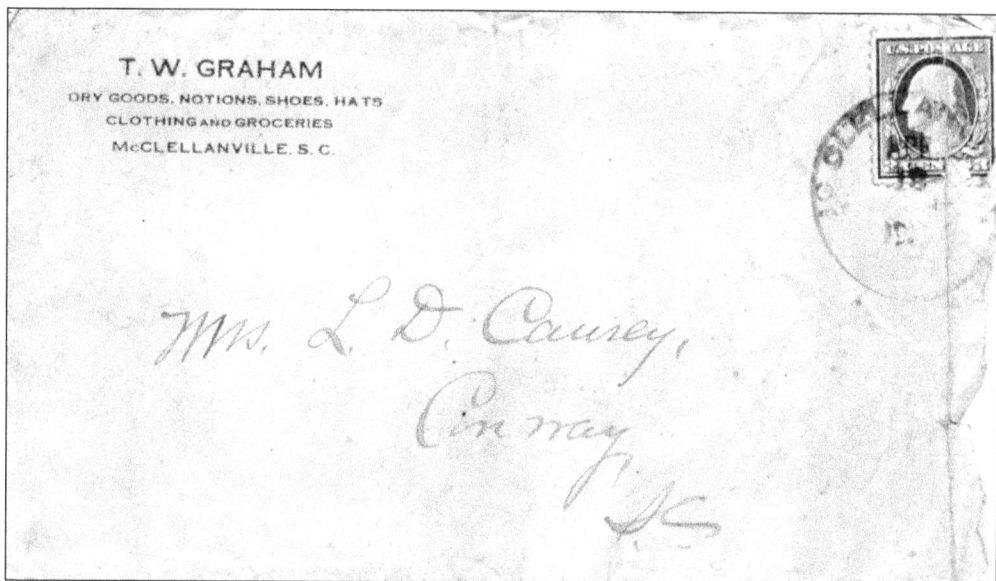

Postmarked McClellanville, a letter from T. W. Graham and Company was mailed to a Conway cousin about 1912. The envelope's return address lists the store's products as dry goods, notions, shoes, hats, clothing, and groceries. Three brothers, T. W. Graham Jr., Francis Graham, and Robert Graham, were partners in this business, which was started by their father, Thomas W. Graham.

Thomas William Graham Jr. (1873–1950) was a local entrepreneur who lived with his wife, Eugenie "Jennie" Isabelle Morrison (1876–1960), at 140 Oak Street. They are seen at the home of his brother, John H. Graham. Their father, Confederate veteran Thomas William Graham Sr. (1849–1905), sold his mercantile interests near Conway in 1887 and bought Woodville and Elmwood Plantations on the South Santee River, relocating from Woodville to McClellanville in 1900.

John Hugh Graham's store, right, and T. W. Graham and Company, below, occupied the same building at 824 Pinckney Street at sequential times. When T. W. Graham and Company moved to 814 Pinckney Street, John H. Graham's store occupied this site. He sold hardware, furniture, farm implements, automobile accessories, and other goods. He was also a lawyer, with an office upstairs, was a state legislator, and lived at 408 Pinckney Street. He taught Sunday school at McClellanville Methodist Church and gave the land for McClellanville Baptist Church. T. W. Graham and Company solicited business by providing free delivery service for telephone orders and free rides home for rural customers making purchases. John Hugh Graham's store sold caskets and provided a delivery truck to move the casket for services, if needed, as there was no local funeral-directory business. (Picture at right courtesy of Thomasine Graham Harvin.)

R. L. Morrison and Sons, Inc., listed as contractors and wharf builders, organized in 1923 and built their commercial office about 1930 at 822 Pinckney Street. Lawyer Thomas P. Morrison simultaneously had an office there, with his hours by appointment during the week and from 9:00 a.m. to noon on Saturdays. The building was elevated after Hurricane Hugo and is currently a residence. (Courtesy of Charleston County Public Library.)

The Red Cross Pharmacy, 824 Pinckney Street, is seen here in the 1930s with the Ward girls sitting at the entrance, holding baby dolls. The pharmacy, which had a soda fountain, was established in 1916 as the enterprise of Dr. J. Alexander Meldau, a physician living at 608 Morrison Street. It occupied the main floor of this two-story downtown building until around 1945.

Dr. John Alexander Meldau (1858–1939) was born in Sumter and obtained a medical degree from the Kentucky School of Medicine. In 1916, he moved his practice to McClellanville and opened the Red Cross Pharmacy. In 1931, the widower Meldau married Hattie Smith Moseley, a Charleston widow with eight surviving children, the four youngest of which lived with the couple at 608 Morrison Street. They are all seen here.

St. John's Missionary Baptist Church, established in 1905 by Rev. A. W. Wright of Georgetown, is an African American church at 219 Cassena Street. It can be viewed from the village's main street, a short distance down the sandy lane, beside 825 Pinckney Street. The sanctuary was built about 1944 under Rev. J. H. Tisdale of Georgetown and replaced a wooden church on this site.

Thomas "Tommy" Ward's Garage, built about 1935 at 829 Pinckney Street, replaced a garage adjoining the Red Cross Pharmacy across the street. This business sold gasoline and had a small automobile-parts store in the front, with a maintenance garage behind it. After closing, the building became the Yellow Shop, housing an art studio and antique-gift gallery. Ward lived at 832 Pinckney Street with his wife, Lula Mae Felder, and their 11 children.

Decayed exterior walls are the remains of John M. Lofton Jr.'s store, built about 1915 at 833 Pinckney Street. Lofton lived at 32 Morrison Court. His general store later housed Sullivan's Meat Market, operated by George Fred Sullivan and his wife, Beulah Lee, who lived diagonally across from here. Cattle raised on a nearby Sullivan farm were butchered to sell as fresh meat cuts.

Col. William Morrison Toomer's house, 838 Pinckney Street, was built about 1870 and was named Fair Oaks. Richard T. Morrison III built this house and left it to Toomer, his adopted son. Later occupants were the Felders and then the Sullivans, who ran a nearby meat market and whose descendants are restoring the house. Removal of front porch trim revealed it was built on tree-trunk piers.

The Helen Beckman Smith house at 841 Pinckney Street was built about 1932 beside her parents' home. She was a daughter of Ludwig A. Beckman and Eugenia Griffin Leland. She married Raymond B. Smith from Georgetown, and the couple had four children, Jeanette Smith, Jean Smith, Raymond Smith Jr., and Essie Smith.

Ludwig Armstrong Beckman's house, 845 Pinckney Street, was built about 1901 on a one-and-one-half-acre lot bordering a Jeremy Creek tributary, Leland Creek. Called "Mr. Lutie," Beckman planted rice at Blackwood Plantation in the Santee Delta and became superintendent of the Santee Gun Club in 1905. A son of William P. Beckman, he married Eugenia Griffin Leland, and they had seven children.

James B. Morrison Jr.'s store, built about 1910 at 852 Pinckney Street, is now a residence. The one-story general merchandise store featured a metal gabled roof over shiplap siding. A gristmill, sawmill, and George Beckman's cotton gin were located in this vicinity in the early 1900s. Morrison lived at 718 Pinckney Street.

McClellanville Oyster Factory, shown here in 1948, was at the junction of Leland and Jeremy Creeks. A second oyster cannery was directly across Jeremy Creek, on Skipper's Point. Two oyster canneries were reportedly operating on Jeremy Creek by 1913, one of which was McClellanville Canning Company, which issued tokens in the early 1900s. Oyster shells were recycled as clutch for new oyster growth and as pavement on village streets.

In 1868, William Peter Beckman relocated his general store from beside the Deerhead Oak to 916 Pinckney Street, where he built a two-and-one-half-story structure with a mercantile store on the main floor and a residence upstairs. Strategic holes in the upstairs floor enabled Beckman to covertly view financial transactions below. This Greek Revival–style house was an antiquities museum during South Carolina's 1970 tercentennial.

The Beckman School House, 936 Pinckney Street, was built about 1875 by William P. Beckman for his children. The main floor was for classes, and the upstairs living quarters were for a teacher. Beckman's son, Ludwig A. Beckman, and his bride began their marriage in this former schoolhouse, at the intersection of Pinckney and South Pinckney Streets. As the young family grew, they built a larger house at 845 Pinckney Street.

The Minnie Beckman Cash house, 941 North Pinckney Street, was built about 1913 as the summer home of R. J. Margarel of New Jersey. A second house, which was later removed from the lot, faced South Pinckney Street, behind this house. "Miss Minnie" was a daughter of George Edward Beckman and lived in the schoolhouse next door before purchasing this home in 1946. She married Fred "Pee Wee" Cash and died without issue.

Around 1936, the Hughes Brothers' Winery, located at North Pinckney Street near Highway 17, made Scuppernong wine. Eugene Hughes and Roland Hughes ran the state-licensed winery in their retirement. The sons of Franklin D. Hughes, they moved here with their family from Conway. Roland Hughes lived in Dr. John S. Palmer's c. 1854 house, which was relocated to 401 Pinckney Street from Palmer's Point, where poet Henry Timrod occupied it as a tutor. The house burned in 1923.

The Ella Skipper Sessions house, 971 South Pinckney Street, was built about 1891 on the headwaters of Jeremy Creek. It stands on what was a 9.97-acre tract Sessions purchased in 1891 for $598 from farmers James W. Coleman and Andrew J. Coleman. Ella married P. G. Sessions, had four children, and rented the DuPre house, 423 Pinckney Street, for several years before moving to North Charleston around 1929 to be near her daughter, Mary Sessions Taylor.

Dr. Edward Archibald McClellan (1872–1944), pictured about 1892, was a son of Lawrence Perry McClellan and Absley Grace Skipper. He married Lucy Pegues (1886–1961) of Cheraw and lived there until returning to McClellanville as a physician in 1907. The couple had four children and lived in a home at 1016 South Pinckney Street, which later burned.

McClellanville Baptist Church, 1064 South Pinckney Street, is seen here on a 1946 postcard. This was the first Baptist church organized between Georgetown and Mount Pleasant. A planning meeting at a local school in 1939 led to Sunday school classes held in New Wappetaw Presbyterian Church. Construction ensued on this building with donated property and materials, and it was finished in 1943.

46

The Fredrick Rutledge Baker house, 234 Baker Street, was built before 1886, the year of Charleston's "Great Shake" earthquake. The house began as a retail store and residence and is the village's oldest brick-veneer building, with brick replacing the original wood siding. Baker was born in 1859 to Dr. W. T. W. Baker and Eliza H. Bacon and married Emma Leland of Walnut Grove Plantation, Awendaw Creek. (Courtesy of Charleston County Public Library.)

The Samuel Leland Baker house, 228 Baker Street, was built about 1913. The same builder constructed similar Craftsman cottages for villagers Rutledge Leland, R. H. Peacock, and David M. Mackintosh within several years. Baker was born in 1884 to Fredrick R. Baker and Emma Leland and built beside his parents' home. He married Elizabeth "Bessie" Toomer Briggs and was a merchant like his father.

McClellanville Library, 222 Baker Street, is the oldest branch of the Charleston County Public Library. It began in the J. Hibben Leland house at 120 Oak Street in 1886 and moved in 1927 to the former village school at Memorial Park on Pinckney Street. The present facility was built as the James E. Scott Jr. Medical Clinic, a public-health center named in memory of a village physician, and became a library in 1983.

John Marion Lofton Jr.'s house, 32 Morrison Court, was built about 1916. A son of John M. Lofton Sr. and Eliza A. Morrison, Lofton was an accountant who ran a passenger and freight boat, the *Atlas*, to and from Charleston until selling it and opening a general store at 833 Pinckney Street. Lofton married Harriet Gadsden Lucas of the Wedge Plantation, South Santee River, and they had four children, including noted author and journalist John M. Lofton (1919–1990). This house remains in the family.

Richard Leland Morrison's house, 12 Morrison Court, was built *c.* 1906. He lived at Doe Hall Plantation, five miles south of McClellanville, and planted rice before organizing R. L. Morrison and Sons. Like his father and a son, Morrison was a state legislator. His marriage to Mary Oswald Freeman yielded three surviving sons. A second marriage was without issue. The house passed to his son Judge James Brown Morrison and remains in his family.

Silver Hill Plantation, across Jeremy Creek from Morrison Court, was the site of an 1862 encampment of 500 Confederate soldiers, who wrote of mosquito-infested misery at Palmer's Point. The land was named for early owner Dr. John Saunders Palmer. This *c.* 1888 house built for Millard F. Skipper at 814 Kit Hall Road derived its name from a silver dollar reportedly placed in its foundation.

Henry Toomer Morrison's creek home, 21 Morrison Avenue, was built in 1900 and burned in 1920. A modern house replaces it. Morrison was a civil engineer, village intendant, or mayor, and son of Richard T. Morrison II. He married Sarah Ward McGillivray, and they raised seven children on this five-acre property, housing an oyster factory and cotton gin. Son William McGillivray Morrison was mayor of Charleston.

Four Morrison family patriarchs in 1948 observed Jeremy Creek, named for patriarch King Jeremy, chief of the Native American tribe that earlier inhabited McClellanville. They are, from left to right, Richard Tillia Morrison III, Henry Toomer Morrison, Richard Leland Morrison, and Robert Hepburn Morrison. Children at this family reunion peer from behind the men.

The Harrington Waddell Morrison Sr. house, 718 Morrison Street, was built about 1922 on nearby Bellefield Plantation, now Thornhill Farm. In 1933, the four-room house was moved to this site, where it has been enlarged. Marble entry steps and an entry-door transom window were incorporated from the c. 1876 Morris Island light keeper's house, previously near Charleston Harbor. Morrison was a partner in R. L. Morrison and Sons, and the house remains in his family.

The creekside Murray/Scott-Cain house, 703 Morrison Street, was built about 1899 by John Osgood Murray as a wedding gift to his wife, Frances M. Webb, a widow with two children. The house was built on a two-acre lot acquired at the time of construction. Murray was vice president of St. James Santee Agricultural Society upon its 1903 reactivation. Dr. James E. Scott Jr., village physician from 1939 to 1957, later lived here.

Dr. James Edward Scott Jr. (1913–1957) moved his family here from Charleston and had a concrete block medical office built at 826 Pinckney Street. He lived at 703 Morrison Street with his wife, Frances Cade, and their three sons. Scott was killed in an automobile accident. A county medical clinic named for him is now the McClellanville Library at 222 Baker Street. His office became Marcos Pharmacy and later a restaurant. Scott is on the right; his friend Binks DuPre is on the left.

The Mary A. Mills house was built about 1890 at 635 Morrison Street. Mary married Levi Eli Mills, assistant head guide for the Santee Gun Club under his father, head guide Charles Mills, and later became head guide for Kinloch Plantation, North Santee River. This 1,520-square-foot house with weatherboard siding has a main-floor bay window facing the sea.

The Tom Duke house, 627 Morrison Street, was built in the late 1930s and is shown here in the 1970s. Originally the office of Livingston's Bulls Bay Seafood Company and a magistrate court when Tom Duke was magistrate, it was relocated to this site and converted to a residence by Beckett and Marie Duke Hills in the 1960s. Renovations have given this house the appearance of a modern home. (Courtesy of Charleston County Public Library.)

The Happy Home, 625 Morrison Street, was one of the houses that James Brown Morrison had built for each of his daughters in the late 19th century. Daughter Susan Morrison, owner of this house, married John Terry Hills, a son of Janie Taber Lofton and George Walter Hills and a superintendent with the Civilian Conservation Corps. This vernacular house with dormer windows was elevated and has had several additions but remains in the family.

Mary Woods "May" Morrison Brailsford's house, 631 Venning Street, was built about 1917, after her larger boarding house, called the Central Hotel, burned on this site. A daughter of Robert V. Morrison and E. Aletha Muldrow, she led a Works Progress Administration effort that employed youths to transplant native trees and vines for town beautification. Mature live oaks beside village streets are the result of her work. She married Robert McLeod Brailsford Jr. and had three children.

Mary W. "May" M. Brailsford (1873–1968) was a schoolteacher and village eccentric, nicknamed "Grandma Moses" for her primitive painting style. Magnolia blooms were a favorite subject, and she gave her botanical paintings as wedding gifts to couples throughout the village. Brailsford also started the local tradition of tolling church bells at midnight each New Year's Eve.

The former New Wappetaw Presbyterian Church manse, 632 Venning Street, was built about 1880 on a lot given by Aletha M. Morrison, widow of Robert V. Morrison. This two-story Folk Victorian house is enhanced by a double-tiered, wraparound porch and a double-tiered bay window. The Presbyterians sold their manse in 2001, and a compatible renovation with addition followed.

The Lucille Morrison Leland Cottage, 622 Venning Street, was built about 1938 on a quiet village street. Their daughter, historian Agnes Leland Baldwin, began her marriage to William P. Baldwin Jr. in this cottage, which later became a rental house. An entry deck and landscaping enhance this property, which contributed to the village historic district's nomination for the National Register of Historic Places. (Courtesy of Charleston County Public Library.)

The R. H. Peacock house, 207 Scotia Street, was built about 1913 on a $300 lot Peacock purchased that year from Ursula Aletha Morrison Mackintosh, widow of David MacNab Mackintosh. Their son, David M. Mackintosh Jr., married Mamie Peacock, daughter of Mr. and Mrs. R. H. Peacock of Rock Hill, who built this house and moved in beside their daughter and son-in-law.

The David MacNab Mackintosh Jr. house, 211 Scotia Street, was also built about 1913. Mackintosh was a son of Ursula Aletha M. Mackintosh and her late husband, who drowned in 1894, when the couple lived on Edisto Island. Mackintosh sold her son the 211 Scotia Street lot and sold his in-laws the 207 Scotia Street lot, so the newlyweds lived between their parents. They moved to Rock Hill with the Peacocks in 1928.

The Eugenia "Jennie" Mackintosh Morrison house, 217 Scotia Street, is a Colonial Revival–style home built about 1939 to replace her mother's home, the c. 1889 Ursula Aletha M. Mackintosh house razed on this site. Mackintosh was a daughter of Robert Venning Morrison and Elizabeth Aletha Muldrow and ran a millinery shop downtown on Pinckney Street. Morrison was Mackintosh's daughter; she married Wells Morrison and had three children.

The Mackintosh cottage at 219 Scotia Street, behind 223 Scotia Street, began as village postmaster James Douglas Mackintosh's art studio in his backyard. He built it about 1959 out of timbers he salvaged by disassembling a building his wife purchased, the former post office and Bank of McClellanville building at 710 Pinckney Street. One of their sons, Stuart Mackintosh, expanded the studio to create a small residence in 1974. (Courtesy of Charleston County Public Library.)

The James Douglas Mackintosh house, 223 Scotia Street, began as a two-room house built before 1900 on a front corner of his lot. Relocated to the present site in exchange for a $10 gold piece, the house received a two-story wing addition in 1925 and a one-story, kitchen-replacement addition in 1971. Mackintosh married Margaret Leslie Michie of Darlington, and they had four children, in whose family the house remains. (Courtesy of Charleston County Public Library.)

Old Bethel African Methodist Episcopal Church, 369 Drayton Street, was built about 1872 by Paul B. Drayton. It was severely damaged by a 1916 hurricane and rebuilt under Rev. S. K. Howard. Replaced by a 1980 sanctuary, the church became a mortuary for Manigault Funeral Home of Georgetown until Hurricane Hugo disabled it. Now stabilized, it is a National Historic Landmark.

The Paul Hamilton Seabrook house was built about 1920 at 226 Oak Street. Seabrook was a son of Archibald H. Seabrook and Caroline P. Seabrook, owners of El Dorado Plantation when it burned in 1897. He was mayor of McClellanville and ran a general-merchandise store in his name at 725 Pinckney Street. He married Apsley Grace Lofton, daughter of Henry M. Lofton Jr. and Caroline M. McClellan.

The John Marion Lofton Sr. house, 218 Oak Street, was built about 1870. Lofton (1845–1927) was a son of Samuel Herd Lofton and Susan Ann Lowry. Orphaned at 12, he joined the 10th Regiment of the South Carolina Militia at 16. After the Civil War, Lofton married Eliza Ann Morrison (1850–1920), and they had nine children. He was a farmer, teacher, postmaster, and state legislator. A post office addition was later removed. (Courtesy of Charleston County Public Library.)

Notable for palmetto-log entrance columns, cypress shingles, and the village's largest hydrangea hedge, the Folk Victorian Henry Michael Lofton Jr. house, 217 Oak Street, was built about 1902 as a wedding gift to his bride, Caroline Matilda McClellan. Lofton, a son of Henry Michael Lofton and Susan Ann Morrison, said of his village, "Once you drink the water, you don't want to leave."

The Clay Travers house, 212 Oak Street, began as military housing at Fort Moultrie on Sullivan's Island. After World War II, the house was purchased by Harry Travers, disassembled, and moved to the edge of his 217 Oak Street lot, formerly Lofton property. Travers reassembled the house for his son, who married Frankie Ellen Graham, daughter of John Hugh Graham and Marie Mitchell. They had two girls, Ellen Travers and Joyce Marie Travers.

Capt. Robert Hepburn Morrison's house, 208 Oak Street, was built about 1896. He was a son of Robert V. Morrison and E. Aletha Muldrow, who lived on this corner, across Venning Street. Morrison and his wife, Ida Briggs Brailsford, were the parents of eight children. An entrance sidelight has the names of some of the children that were etched in glass with a diamond engagement ring by the oldest child, Ida Morrison, in 1914.

Capt. R. Hepburn Morrison (1871–1964) was a lumberman and piloted the *Spray*, a freight and passenger boat. He had a harrowing experience in 1900, when he and a sailor were on a sailboat that shipwrecked in a storm. The sailor could not swim and eventually drowned. Morrison finally drifted and swam to Bulls Island, where he passed out and later awakened and crawled to the lighthouse for aid.

St. James Santee Chapel of Ease Episcopal Church, 205 Oak Street, was built in 1891 by Paul B. Drayton and replaced Brick Church on Old Kings Highway in 1912. The Victorian Gothic chapel was designed by Alexander H. Lucas. It was constructed of longleaf pine and cypress with a cupola on its steep roof and fronts Church Street. Charlotte A. Cordes Doar gave the property, and Mary Stewart Pinckney provided major construction funding.

A Shuler couple from Holly Hill built the c. 1900 house shown behind them at 221 Charlotte Street. They later sold the house and moved away. The house belonged to Mrs. Edward P. McClellan in 1926, when she loaned the main floor for a new community center, the Greenlawn Playhouse. However, within months, a fire started at the popular playhouse, which burned this house and two others nearby. (Courtesy of Thomasine Graham Harvin.)

The Martha Gillison Doar house, 208 Charlotte Street, was built about 1928 on a lot conveyed by her mother, Sarah B. Doar, whose larger home adjoins the property. The owner was born in 1885, a spinster daughter of Samuel Cordes Doar. Called Mattie Manor for its resident, this bungalow floated off its foundation during Hurricane Hugo and was restored where it settled. (Courtesy of Charleston County Public Library.)

Charlotte Ann Cordes Doar's Big House was built about 1875 at 203–205 Charlotte Street, next to Beckman's Beach, a favorite creek shoreline for swimming. Doar married Stephen Duval Doar, and their main home was the South Santee River plantation in Harrietta. This house, shown in 1909, burned in the 1926 fire started in the Greenlawn Playhouse. Pinckney Cottage, 519 Pinckney Street, and the house hosting the playhouse also burned.

Five village children related as siblings or cousins appear ready for a creek swim around 1920. They are, from left to right, Billy Leland, Bobby Graham, Lyda Graham, Rutledge "Wewa" Leland Jr., and Jim Leland. The gentle pace of their village childhood may have contributed to their longevity, for the oldest four swimmers celebrated 90th birthdays in recent years.

Young Anthony DuPre and Ted "Tin-Tin" Barrett practice rowing in Jeremy Creek during the 1940s. Growing up in a creek village gave local youths countless opportunities for a mariner's education as they played in Jeremy Creek under the watchful eyes of village boat captains and crews, often their family or neighbors.

The Sarah Butler Doar house, 204 Charlotte Street, was built about 1905. She married Samuel Cordes Doar and received the property from her mother-in-law, Charlotte A. Cordes Doar, whose substantial home was at 203–205 Charlotte Street, which was named for her. Now the village's largest historic home at 3,528 square feet, this house remains in the Doar-Prentiss family.

Arthur Orlando Atkinson's house, built about 1894 at 559 Water Street, was beside the site of the burned c. 1869 home of Dr. W. T. W. Baker, Confederate surgeon and village physician. Archibald J. McClellan sold Baker his lot on a Jeremy Creek slough for $350 in 1870. Born on Oakton Plantation, Georgetown County, Atkinson was a Confederate veteran who acquired his lot parcel from Samuel Lofton, who bought it from the widow Susan L. Baker.

Dr. William Thomas Wilkins Baker (1825–1894) graduated from the medical college in Charleston and practiced medicine in Sumter until relocating his practice to this area around 1860. He married Eliza Henrietta Bacon, and they had eight children. Four years after his wife's 1870 death, Baker married Susan Anna Leland (1851–1927) and had a daughter, Elizabeth. He later became a state legislator.

The Robert V. Morrison house, 144 Oak Street, was built about 1860. Morrison was a planter who married Elizabeth Aletha Muldrow, and they raised 11 children in this home, which now belongs to the St. James Santee Chapel of Ease Episcopal Church and serves as a place for parish functions and Sunday school classes. Several carefully planned renovations have allowed the house to retain historic character.

Robert Venning Morrison (1842–1924) and Elizabeth Aletha Muldrow (1848–1937) were married in 1865, following his Civil War service. Their Oak Street home was built for Reddin Baxley, a South Santee River postmaster who purchased one of the first village lots sold and built what is now its third oldest house. Morrison's family gave land for the Presbyterian church and manse, the Masonic lodge, and the present school.

The Eugenie "Jennie" Morrison Graham house, 140 Oak Street, was built about 1904 and features elements of Folk Victorian and Queen Anne architecture. Of particular note are its decorative eave brackets. The house was built for Graham and her husband, local merchant Thomas W. Graham Jr. The couple had eight children, in whose families the house remains. (Courtesy of Charleston County Public Library.)

Charlton Henry Leland's house, 126 Oak Street, was built about 1888 after his parents, J. Hibben Leland and Susan A. Morrison, conveyed a portion of their adjoining property to him. Leland (1855–1922) married Louise Augusta Lofton (1867–1956), daughter of Henry Michael Lofton and Susan Ann Morrison, and they had four children. The house passed to the oldest child, Louise Leland, who married George Stroman, and it remains in the family.

Doar Cottage, previously Whilden Cottage, faces the creek at 125 Oak Street. It was built about 1862 on property Louis Augustus Whilden purchased that year from Richard T. Morrison II for $100. The home was renamed for its subsequent owner, Dr. Stephen Decatur Doar, a village physician who treated patients in a small outbuilding behind the house. A kitchen building also survived, along with this fourth oldest village house that belongs to a Doar descendant.

Dr. Stephen Decatur Doar (1838–1923) was a son of Stephen Duval Doar and Charlotte Ann Cordes. He graduated from Yale and from the medical college in Charleston. The Confederate surgeon married Jane E. Gadsden and planted rice at Harrietta Plantation on the South Santee River. They had eight children. A second marriage to Harriott Rutledge Toomer was without issue. (Courtesy of Mary Lucas Easley.)

Capt. Louis Augustus Whilden 1832-1864

Capt. Louis Augustus Whilden (1832–1864) descended from John Whilden II, the first land grant recipient of McClellanville property in 1705. He married Sarah Claudia Morrison (1838–1922), the eldest child of Richard T. Morrison II and Elizabeth A. Venning, and they had two children. Captain Whilden distinguished himself at death in the Civil War and was buried beside the former Wappetaw Independent Church in Awendaw.

James Hibben Leland's house, 120 Oak Street, was built about 1858 and is the second oldest village home. The Huguenot cottage received the first of several additions in 1887. Five Leland generations lived here, where the first village library organized in 1886 and the St. James Cotillion was held annually. Leland fought in the Pee Dee Light Artillery of the Civil War and was postmaster, parish magistrate, and the first village schoolteacher.

Eliza Hibben Leland Morrison (1847–1923) was born to J. Hibben Leland (1810–1892) and Susan Ann Morrison (1818–1903). Her grandfathers were a Mount Pleasant founder, Capt. James Hibben, and Rev. Dr. Aaron Whitney Leland, minister of First Scots Presbyterian Church in Charleston. She married James Brown Morrison and had 10 children. Here she is seated by the "dock," a bridged slough paralleling Oak Street that was a safe boat harbor in storms.

The Rutledge Baker Leland house, 119 Oak Street, was built about 1916 on a knoll forming the creek-front property of his childhood home, 120 Oak Street. It was accessed via a bridged slough, which was later covered. The knoll was enlarged by back-filling retaining walls with dredge spoil. Seated on the porch around 1940 is Leland's wife, Claudia Lucille Morrison, a daughter of James Brown Morrison and Eliza Hibben Leland.

Robert Jack McCarley (left) and Rutledge B. Leland display a row of ducks. This picture may have been taken in 1923 when the State newspaper reported that McCarley had been deer and duck hunting with Leland in November. These men married daughters of James Brown Morrison, and McCarley's son later bought the home at 114 Oak Street, opposite that of his uncle Rutledge Leland.

Dr. Horace W. Leland's house was built about 1875 at 114 Oak Street. It was a summer home for the Leland family of Walnut Grove Plantation on Awendaw Creek and passed to a spinster daughter, Mary Claudia Leland, who partitioned it into 13 boarding rooms around 1900 and named it the Seaside Inn. Called "Aunt Mamie," Mary Leland ran the inn until she died in 1935, after which it sold and was returned to a private residence. (Courtesy of Dr. Walter Bonner.)

Dr. Horace Wells Leland (1820–1885) was a son of Rev. Dr. Aaron W. Leland and Elizabeth Hibben. He was educated at South Carolina College and the medical college in Charleston. Leland and his wife, Eugenia Rebecca Griffin, had 11 children. A Confederate surgeon, Leland purchased Walnut Grove Plantation from David Doar around 1874 and lived there, growing tobacco and cotton. This is his grave marker in the village cemetery; no known pictures of him exist.

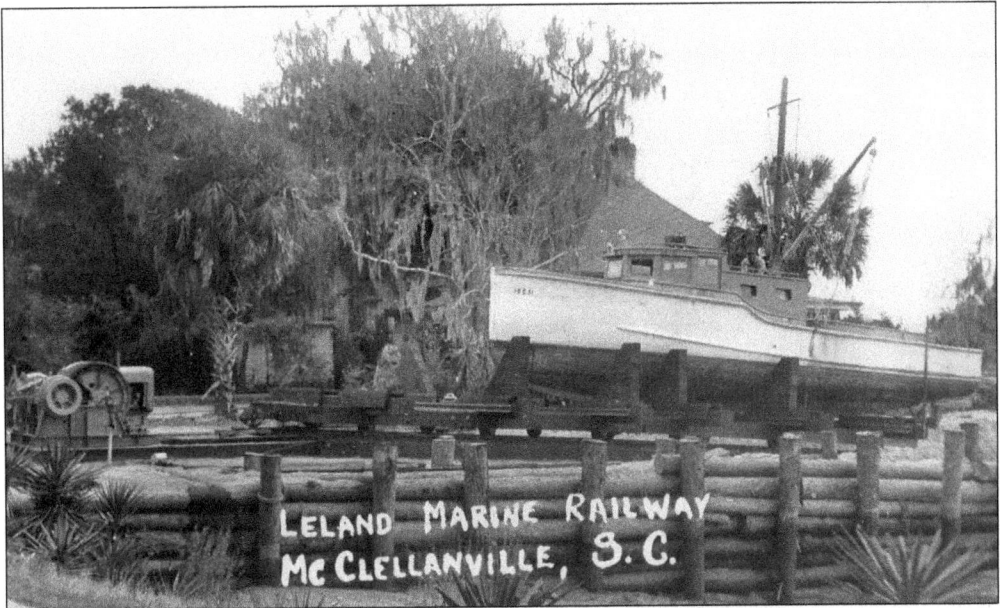

Leland Marine Railway, 115 Oak Street, was a large boat launch installed during the heyday of McClellanville's boat traffic in the 20th century. Here the *Shirley Ann*, which belonged to Giradeau Leland, is shown. The rails are relocated up the creek at the docking facilities of R. L. Morrison and Sons. In the last three decades, shrimp boats operating from Jeremy Creek have decreased from 50 to about a dozen.

Point Pleasant Inn, built before 1862 and moved to one of the village's earliest developed lots at 108 Oak Street, was the summer home of Richard T. Morrison II. It passed to his spinster daughter, Mary Belle Morrison, who told of its move from Tibwin Plantation after her infant brother's death. She ran a boarding house here after 1910. The house was razed after Morrison's death in 1968 to build a modern home, which remains in the family.

73

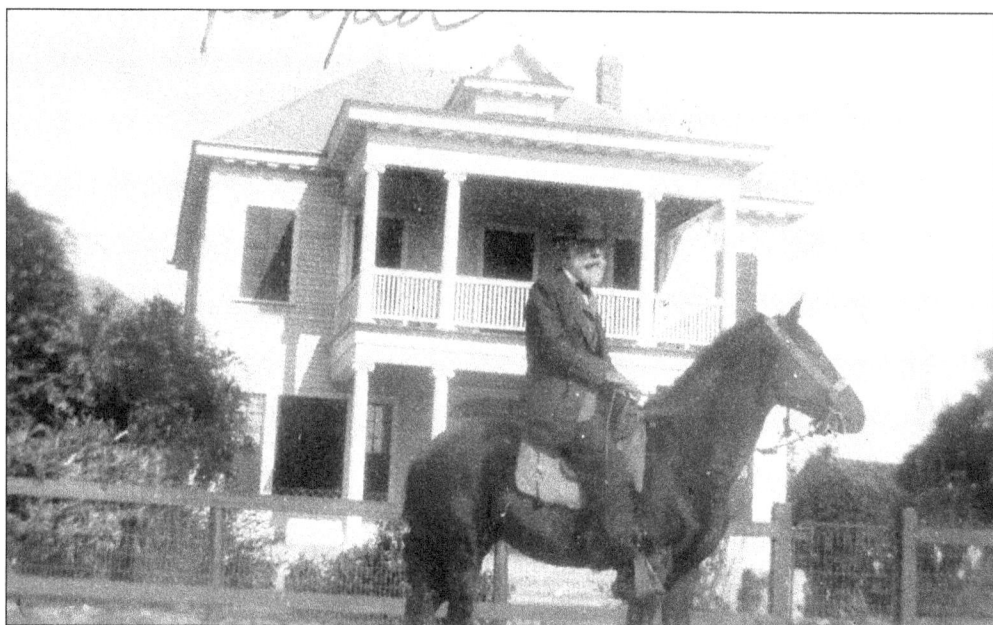

Ursula Bonneau Morrison McGillivray's house, 102 Oak Street, was built about 1920 overlooking Jeremy Creek. She was a daughter of Richard T. Morrison II and Eliza A. Toomer and married Dr. Hugh Swinton McGillivray, chairman of the English department at the Citadel, in Charleston. They had two children. James Brown Morrison is shown here on horseback in front of McGillivray's house. (Courtesy of Lyda Graham.)

Dr. J. Alexander Meldau's house, 608 Morrison Street, was built about 1910 by neighbor Ursula B. McGillivray and called the New Cottage. McGillivray sold her cottage and a one-eighth-acre lot to Clarence Lawton Anderson in 1914 for $1,225. Meldau bought it in 1916, after moving here to practice medicine and open a pharmacy. Upon his death, it sold to John Allen Solomons and his wife, Aletha Graham, in whose family it remains.

Turpentine Still.

A similar turpentine distillery owned by a Pittman family from Georgia operated at the end of Oak Street beside Jeremy Creek a century ago. Others were scattered in the parish, as naval store production of tar, pitch, and turpentine fueled the local economy, along with cotton, after the decline of rice production. The site is now occupied by McClellanville's seafood industries, with shrimp boats docked near wholesale and retail seafood markets.

Turpentine production was prevalent locally after the Civil War because of abundant pine forests and convenient harvesting methods. A man could be a successful turpentiner without slave labor. This c. 1905 stereoview shows an African American man slashing a pine tree's bark with a tool called a hack. A container attached below the slash collected sap for distillation processing.

75

Shrimpers of Portuguese and Greek origin who trawled off the Gulf Coast of Florida temporarily relocated to McClellanville in the 1930s. Their success introduced commercial shrimping locally, but few images of the foreigners survived. This painting depicts Luis Menendez's shrimp boat, *Vacio de Gama*, in 1935. Shrimping became a leading local industry after World War II, when village soldiers came home to shrimp.

The shrimp boat *Geneva Moore* was built about 1905 in Swansboro, North Carolina, and named for the wife of its first captain, Alex Moore. It relocated here from Charleston in 1926, and villager Joe Cumbee became the last owner of this shrimp boat, for which a village street is named. U.S. Coast Guard lieutenant commander Tyree Moore, stationed in Charleston during World War II, heard about a village boat with his mother's name and came to rediscover his father's old boat.

The first airplane landing in a village pasture on December 28, 1919, created great excitement in McClellanville. The biplane's pilot took a few villagers for a spin before departing and was undoubtedly the talk of the town for weeks. Georgetown County Airport on Highway 17, about 20 miles north of the village, is the closest commercial airport.

Wild Flower Tourist Camp, on the Ocean Hiway, U. S. 17, near McClellanville, South Carolina

Wildflower Tourist Camp was a c. 1940s Highway 17 roadside motel, one-and-one-half-miles south of McClellanville, where McClellanville Diner exists now. Accommodations included a Texaco gas station, luncheon restaurant, and six "modern" cottages with the latest sleeping comfort, Beautyrest mattresses. Some cabins had two separate units, and one resembled a log cabin.

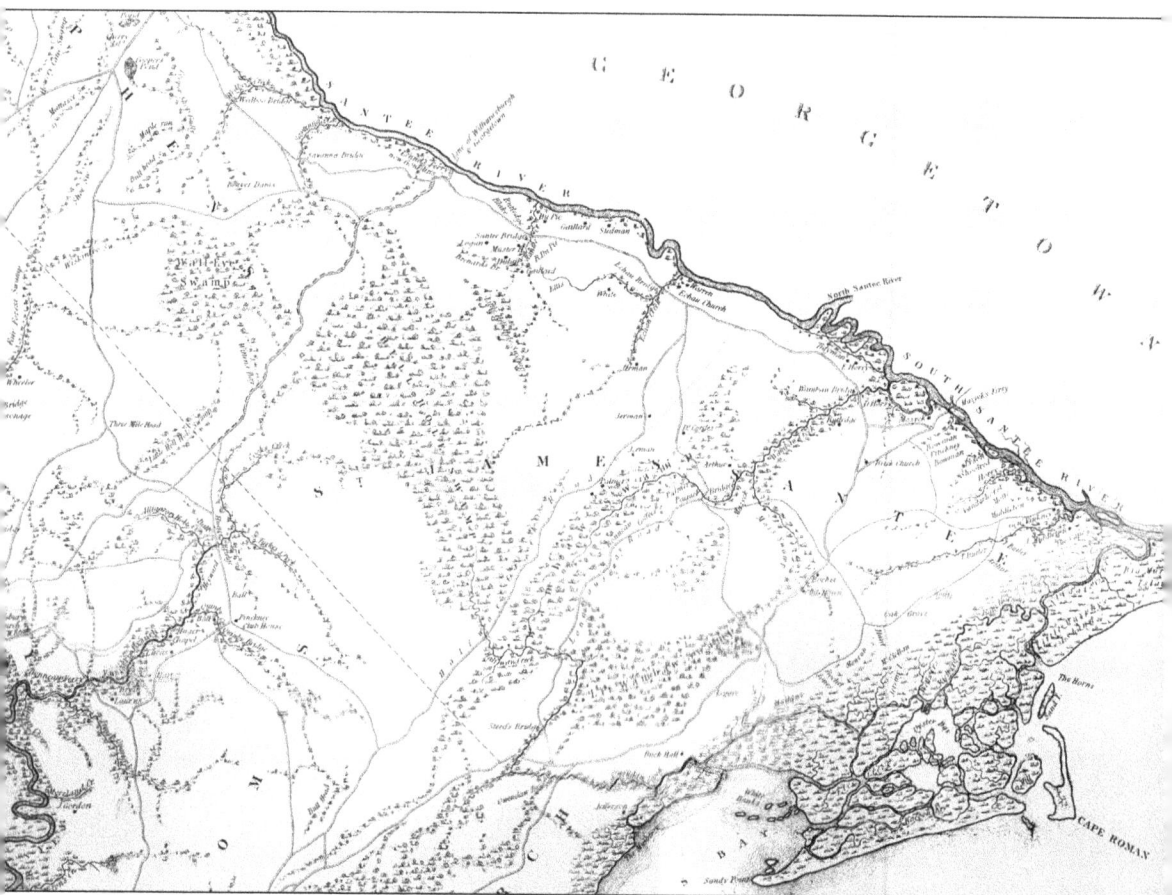

An 1820 map of St. James, Santee Parish, excerpted from the Charleston District map prepared from surveys by Charles Vignoles and Henry Ravenel, was improved for publication in Robert Mills's 1825 atlas of South Carolina. It shows parish boundaries, which currently correspond to the South Santee River on the north, Awendaw and Steed Creeks on the south, the Intracoastal Waterway on the east, and Highway 41 on the west. Surnames on the map denote family residences. Robert Mills was the state engineer and architect when he ordered this map prepared, and he later assumed a similar position with the federal government. His designs included the Fireproof Building in Charleston, numerous South Carolina courthouses, and the Washington Monument in the District of Columbia.

Two

PARISH PLANTATIONS AND CHURCHES

St. James Santee Episcopal Church, also Brick Church or Wambaw Church, was built about 1768 on Old Kings Highway, six miles south of the South Santee River. This fourth parish church retains original hand-hewn cypress pews and flagstone tiles, but its altar was destroyed during the Revolutionary and Civil Wars. Nearby gravestones recall its distinguished membership. (Courtesy of South Carolina Historical Society.)

A c. 1930 interior view of St James Santee Episcopal Church reveals Palladian windows, a cove ceiling, and crown molding—all enhancing this rural parish church. The church also had a chancel at the northern sanctuary wall, relocated from its eastern wall. The architect of this church, which served English and French parishioners, is unknown. It is a National Historic Landmark. (Courtesy of South Carolina Historical Society.)

A cypress swamp bordering Old Kings Highway between St. James Santee Episcopal Church and the South Santee River ferry landing is pictured here in this c. 1930s photograph. Majestically tall cypress and tupelo gum trees stand in dark water quietly teeming with wildlife. Naturalist writer Archibald Rutledge may have drawn literary inspiration from this swamp, near his country home, Hampton Plantation. Also, naturalist artist John James Audubon likely visited here when he was a

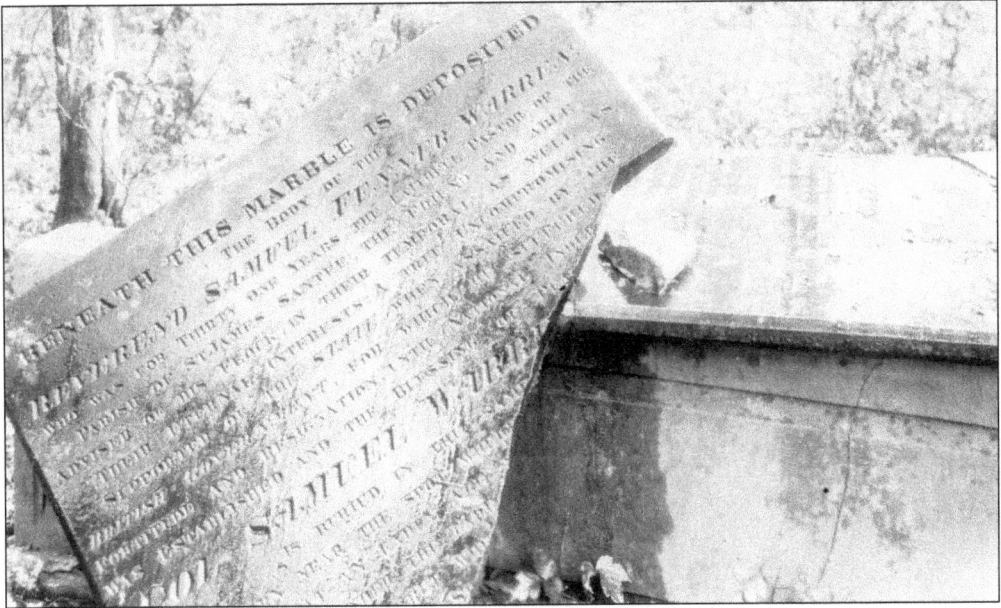

Rev. Samuel Fenner Warren's grave tablet was broken by 1930. Warren was rector of St. James Santee Episcopal Church from 1758 to 1788. He married Elizabeth Perdreau, and she died in 1765. Beginning at the nonextant Echaw Church, Warren served the parish during construction of Brick Church. His South Santee River home, Echaw Grove Plantation, was later the site of Battery Warren, a Confederate fort. (Courtesy of South Carolina Historical Society.)

Hampton guest while hunting the Santee region and painting his American bird series. This swamp was most likely on El Dorado Plantation and was similar to the Washo Reserve, which was created by damming Washo Creek on Blake's Plantation to provide a rice-field water supply. The reserve is accessible to the public via a boardwalk at Santee Coastal Reserve Wildlife Management Area off Highway 17 near the South Santee River. (Courtesy of South Carolina Historical Society.)

Hampton Plantation, on the South Santee River tributary of Wambaw Creek in Hampton Plantation State Park, 1950 Rutledge Road, is open daily. Built about 1735 for French Huguenot Noe Serre, it has been home to the prominent South Carolina families of Horry, Pinckney, and Rutledge. Gen. Francis Marion sought respite here during the American Revolution until the British came, and he hastily swam to a nearby island. (Courtesy of South Carolina Historical Society.)

Archibald Hamilton Rutledge (1883–1973), left, graduated from Union College in New York and taught English at Mecersburg Academy in Pennsylvania. He married Florence Hart and had three sons, pictured here beside him. After his wife's death, Rutledge married in 1937 a childhood sweetheart, Alice Lucas of the Wedge Plantation, and retired to his ancestral Hampton Plantation, where the poet and author of nearly 50 books kindly received guests until his last years.

African Americans demonstrate rice pounding at Hampton Plantation in 1936. Archibald Rutledge, South Carolina's first poet laureate, sold Hampton's manor and 322 of its 1,200 acres to the state of South Carolina in 1971 for $150,000 to secure its preservation. It is a National Historic Landmark. Rutledge was eulogized for his generosity and literary genius when buried near Hampton.

Hampton Plantation's kitchen building, built about 1880, is a single-story structure with dual entrances. Plantation kitchens were typically separate buildings to prevent grease fires from burning the main house. Archaeological investigations in the 1990s revealed abandoned brick drain troughs and a brick-lined well beneath this kitchen floor. A c. 1809 kitchen earlier occupied the site, which now houses a rare bat species. (Courtesy of South Carolina Historical Society.)

Edward Rutledge (1749–1800) and John Rutledge were sons of Irish emigrant Dr. John Rutledge and delegates to the First Continental Congress. Edward Rutledge returned to Philadelphia in 1776 and signed the Declaration of Independence. John Rutledge became president and then governor of South Carolina. His son, Frederick Rutledge, married Harriott Horry in 1797, and Hampton Plantation passed to the Rutledges. (Courtesy of Dr. Frank Sanders.)

EDWARD RUTLEDGE.

Eliza Lucas Pinckney (1722–1793) refined the extraction of blue dye from the leaves and flowers of the indigo plant, to the enrichment of Colonial planters. The wife of Charles Pinckney, she was living with her widowed daughter, Harriott Pinckney Horry of Hampton Plantation, when George Washington visited in 1791. She was also the mother of patriot statesmen Thomas Pinckney and Charles Cotesworth Pinckney. No images of Pinckney survived; this is a re-creation.

The rice mill on Waterhorn (earlier spelled Wattahan) Plantation on the South Santee River was the second rice mill built by Jonathan Lucas. It was housed in a two-story structure with an exterior siding of cypress shingles. The plantation belonged to Elias Horry IV (1733–1834), who left it to his second wife. It adjoined Hampton Plantation and later belonged to the Rutledge family. Shown here in 1930, this site is in Francis Marion National Forest. (Courtesy of South Carolina Historical Society.)

An 1802 rice mill diagram explains its action. Water pressure created by raising a floodgate (outside) rotated the axle (left, center), which turned a series of cogwheels to power millstones and pestles. First rice was funneled from a hopper to the lower millstone. Rice was then ground between two millstones and dropped to a wind-fan bin, which rejected hulls and dropped rice to a lower bin. Eight pestles (left, bottom) pounded the rice. Conveyor belts later improved this process.

Pineland was the summer residence of Ballsdam Plantation, a South Santee River plantation belonging to Dr. John Saunders Palmer (1804–1881) and later to his son, Philip Gendron Palmer (1844–1922). The Palmers first occupied Pineland in 1835, though it is not known if their five-room house was built or reconditioned at that time. Buildings shown below include, from left to right, a log cabin made air-tight to protect its musical organ, a small school building, and Dr. Palmer's office and drugstore, which was attached to the visible end of his unadorned, elongated residence (above). Other outbuildings included a birthing house (for child deliveries), stables, a plantation office, and a barn. Pineland was abandoned after the Palmers left the parish, and this property, on high ground near Honey Hill, was acquired by the federal government for Francis Marion National Forest. (Courtesy of South Carolina Historical Society.)

Howard African Methodist Episcopal Church, 2024 Rutledge Road, was founded in 1880, and retains portions of its original building after two moves. It is named for Rev. John Howard, who organized the church and served as its first minister. The church is in Germantown, a freedman's village for descendants of slaves from nearby Santee River plantations.

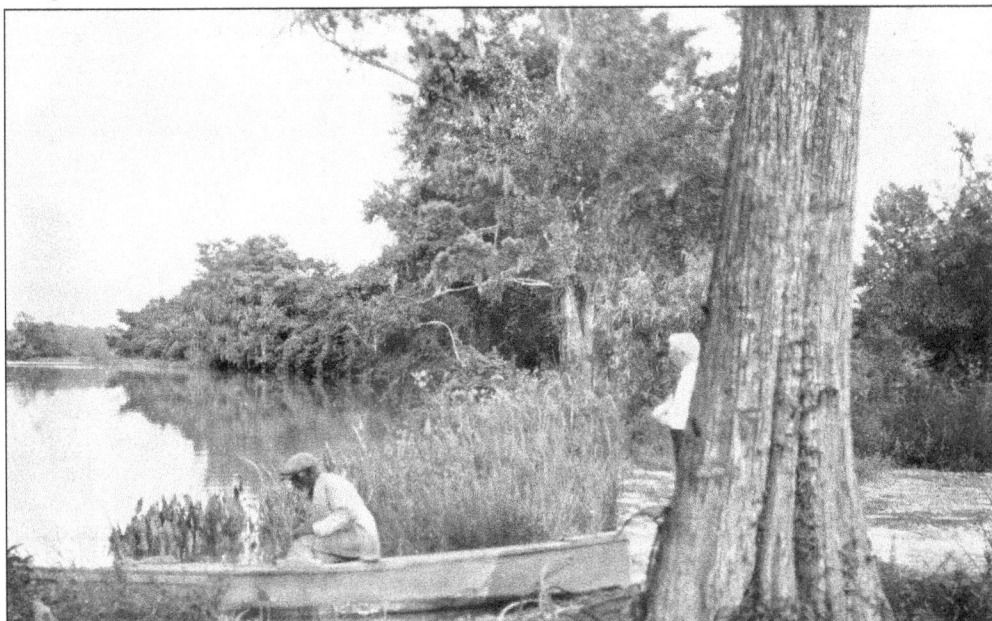

An African American ferry operator, possibly with a surname of Garrett or Jones, from nearby Germantown observes Wambaw Creek by Hampton Plantation and near Waterhorn Ferry landing about 1930. The Santee River and its Catawba and Wateree River tributaries drain approximately 538 miles or 40 percent of South Carolina. The Santee was dammed about 1940 by the state-owned utility company Santee Cooper to create hydroelectric power. (Courtesy of South Carolina Historical Society.)

Peachtree Plantation, on the South Santee River, was built about 1762 for Thomas Lynch Sr., who in 1772 transferred it to Thomas Lynch Jr. and his bride, Elizabeth Shubrick, who lived there until disappearing at sea without issue in 1779. It passed to John Lynch Bowman, a nephew who changed his legal name to John Bowman Lynch to qualify as a Lynch heir. The house, shown here as ruins in 1930, burned in 1846. (Courtesy of South Carolina Historical Society.)

Thomas Lynch Jr. (1749–1779), a signer of the Declaration of Independence, was born at Hopsewee Plantation on the North Santee River and left at age 13 to attend school in England. He returned at age 23 to a home his father built in his absence, Peachtree Plantation, now part of Santee Coastal Reserve Wildlife Management Area. Lynch was a captain of the Provincial Troops and served in the Provincial and Continental Congresses. (Courtesy of Dr. Frank Sanders.)

At the time of this photograph, in the 1970s, pointed timbers protruding from the South Santee riverbank and scattered bricks were the only visible remains of Jonathan Lucas's first water-powered rice mill, which was built about 1787 at Peachtree Plantation. His invention, which streamlined rice milling, was housed near the South Santee River Highway 17 Bridge and also near the plantation house ruins. (Courtesy of Charleston County Public Library.)

Jonathan Lucas (1754–1821) brought the industrial revolution to St. James, Santee Parish with his invention of a water-powered rice mill that minimized the manual labor requirements of separating rice from its hull. Slaves then had more time for other tasks, and overall plantation productivity improved significantly. (Courtesy of Dr. Jonathan Lucas Dieter.)

The Peachtree Oak, once South Carolina's largest live oak tree, with a circumference approaching 32 feet, was the reported source of its plantation's name. The oak's shade canopy covered almost an acre, making it a frequent gathering site for outdoor religious services, which resulted in the name "Preachtree," later modified to Peachtree. The oak was diseased by the 1930s, at the time of this photograph, and it later died. (Courtesy of South Carolina Historical Society.)

Stepne (last name possibly Pinckney) lived in the African American community of Germantown near the South Santee River in the 1930s and 1940s. A skilled hunter, he was knowledgeable of where quail were plentiful and safe to shoot in the Collins Creek area. The Graham brothers and other hunters from McClellanville sought Stepne's advice and returned after hunting to share quail and enjoy a cup of coffee with their advisor. (Courtesy of Frances Garrison Graham.)

Santee River Road was well traveled around 1930. Paralleling the river and connecting its planter families, the road's prominence grew as land transportation surpassed river travel. Most planters' houses originally faced the water, but land entrances were enhanced and sometimes converted to primary entrances as travel evolved. Fairfield Plantation is an example of this revision. (Courtesy of South Carolina Historical Society.)

Big Cypress at Webb's Bridge Santee River Road.

An African American man raises a wooden trunk gate to flood a rice field in this c. 1905 South Carolina stereoview. The Santee Delta, with embanked fields maintained by slaves to maximize crops, was ideal for tidewater rice cultivation. The end of slavery, hurricane-damaged rice dikes, and competition from mechanized rice plantations in the Mississippi River basin signaled the end of Carolina Gold rice.

Fairfield Plantation was built about 1730 by Thomas Lynch Sr. on the first high bluff of the South Santee River's approach. It sold to Jacob Motte and Rebecca Brewton Motte and passed to Thomas Pinckney when he married their daughter, Elizabeth Motte. Pinckney left it to his son, Charles Cotesworth Pinckney, who later passed it to his son, Capt. Thomas Pinckney. This 3,540-square-foot house is the oldest Santee River plantation and is a National Historic Landmark. Fairfield and Peachtree Plantations, along with the North Santee River's Hopsewee Plantation, were all built with Thomas Lynch's indigo fortune. His family was second to the Middletons of Charleston as the wealthiest Colonial South Carolinians. (Courtesy of Charleston County Public Library.)

Thomas Pinckney (1750–1828), was a statesman planter of Fairfield and El Dorado Plantations. The Revolutionary War major also served in the War of 1812, earning the rank of major general. A son of Charles Pinckney and Eliza Lucas Pinckney, he negotiated the "Pinckney Treaty" as an envoy to Spain, was a minister to England, and was governor of South Carolina. (Courtesy of Dr. Frank Sanders.)

The land side of Fairfield Plantation and front of the house reveals its architectural enhancements, such as matching bay windows balancing the entrance portico. Like Hampton Plantation, this house was enlarged several times and has false windows for exterior symmetry. The bay windows and porches were additions, as were several second-floor rooms, which squared the house and created two full stories. (Courtesy of Charleston County Public Library.)

The Wedge Plantation on the South Santee
River is a two-and-one-half-story Greek Revival–
style house built about 1826 by William Lucas,
son of rice-milling pioneer Jonathan Lucas.
Featured on this book's cover, the 1,500-acre
plantation has a 20-room manor house and is
on the National Register of Historic Places.
The name derives from its pie-shaped property.
(Courtesy of South Carolina Historical Society.)

John Marion Lofton Jr. married Harriet Gadsden Lucas of the Wedge Plantation. Here five of
his sisters pose with their husbands around 1930 on the Wedge's steps. They are, from left to
right, George Lunz with Minnie Lofton Lunz, Walter Allen Moore with Abby Lofton Moore,
Julius Seabrook with Gertrude Lofton Seabrook, George Walter Hills with Janie Lofton Hills,
and Alfred Glover Trenholm with Ethel Lofton Trenholm.

A brick slave cabin on the Wedge Plantation, shown in the 1970s, was a double house with a central chimney. Each cabin unit typically contained two small bedrooms and a larger room with a fireplace. Slave quarters were normally wooden structures; brick indicated greater affluence, and this brick cabin is representative of planter William Lucas's enormous wealth. (Courtesy of Charleston County Public Library.)

An early automobile departs the Wedge Plantation, known for extensive gardens of azaleas, camellias, magnolias, live oaks, and flowering bulbs. The manor house was built of cypress and features Italian-marble fireplaces, mahogany stair balustrades, deep wainscoting, and plaster cornices. Original owner William Lucas married Charlotte Hume of Hopsewee Plantation, and they had 10 children. (Courtesy of South Carolina Historical Society.)

In 1888, Leila Waring penned a drawing of Woodville Plantation, which burned in 1900. Its acreage was later absorbed into the adjoining Wedge Plantation. Thomas W. Graham of Conway purchased Woodville in 1887 and moved his family here. He ran a combined general store and the Santee Post Office on Woodville grounds until the fire, after which the family and store were moved to McClellanville. (Courtesy of Lyda Graham.)

Harrietta Plantation, on the South Santee River, was started in 1797 for Harriott Horry Rutledge but not occupied until 1858 when purchased by Stephen Duval Doar and his wife, Charlotte Ann Cordes. Five guest cottages were added about 1930, after the plantation became a waterfowl-hunting retreat restored by wealthy Northerners Horatio and Sophie Shonnard. It is on the National Register of Historic Places. (Courtesy of South Carolina Historical Society.)

David Doar (1850–1928), left, son of Stephen D. Doar and Charlotte A. Cordes, inherited Harrietta Plantation in 1872 and was the Santee River's last large-scale, commercial rice planter. He is pictured with his son, David Doar Jr., center, and his brother, Samuel C. Doar, right. David Doar married Harriett A. Gadsden in 1873, and she died six years later. He then married Sarah R. Walker in 1892 and was survived by five children. (Courtesy of Mary Lucas Easley.)

Magnolia blooms on chintz draperies suggested this bedroom's name following Harrietta Plantation's c. 1930 restoration. The Cherokee rose room, the wild flower room, the pond lily room, and the old mill room were each named for their drapery fabric designs. Harrietta had such a tenuous beginning that some rooms were not plastered until the Shonnard restoration, 133 years after construction began.

The drawing room of Harrietta Plantation, shown after its 1930 renovation, was tastefully appointed with period antiques, family memorabilia, and comfortable upholstered seating. The Adam-style mantle is original to the house. An Aubusson carpet and an antique crystal chandelier enhance the room's decor.

Harrietta Plantation's rice fields are handsomely framed in a brick arch beneath the stately mansion on this plantation of nearly 12,000 acres. The linear house was designed for cross-ventilation, with single-room widths. Harrietta features Greek Revival and Federal-period design elements, is on the National Register of Historic Places property, and is one of only four surviving South Santee River plantation houses. (Courtesy of Charleston County Public Library.)

The design of El Dorado Plantation, built about 1797–1807, is credited to owner Thomas Pinckney, in consultation with his second wife, Frances Motte Middleton, and her mother, Rebecca Brewton Motte. Motte was a Revolutionary War heroine because she allowed her Congaree plantation to be fired upon to extricate the British garrisoned there. She was Pinckney's mother-in-law twice, as he first married another one of her daughters, Elizabeth Motte. (Courtesy of South Carolina Historical Society.)

El Dorado Plantation ruins lie in the 24,000-acre Santee Coastal Reserve Wildlife Management Area on the South Santee River. The house burned about 1897, when inhabited by Archibald Hamilton Seabrook, his wife, Caroline C. Pinckney, and their three youngest children. Fire also claimed Samuel C. Doar's nearby Palo Alto Plantation in 1926. Indian Field and Romney were other area plantations that burned. (Courtesy of South Carolina Historical Society.)

Handwritten annotations around the top photograph: at the one end of the avenue of alternating live-oak, laurel (magnolia) & holly, near the residence at El dorado Santee. Stands to his very large live oak. (The Oakatzi, oracle of 16??) There may be 20 or more symmetrical branches curving upward from its perfect...

A live oak tree at El Dorado Plantation had over 20 branches radiating from its ancient trunk. Photographed about 1930, this magnificent tree was near the South Santee River. A live oak is unusual in that its canopy width can exceed its height, and the species has a life span exceeding 1,000 years. (Courtesy of South Carolina Historical Society.)

A family cemetery is the most visible historic feature of Palmetto Plantation on Dupre Road, north of McClellanville. A modern house replaced 18th- and 19th-century homes built on the property, earlier called Shokes Plantation and DuPre Plantation. William H. Wells sold it in the early 1800s to Methodist minister Daniel DuPre, a signer of the Ordinance of Secession, in whose family it remains.

Laurel Hill Plantation is five miles south of McClellanville, near the Intracoastal Waterway. It was built about 1852 with mortise-and-tenon construction for Richard T. Morrison II. The one-and-one-half-story house was moved from Highway 17 in 1983 and restored by a Morrison descendant. This property, on National Register of Historic Places, was destroyed by Hurricane Hugo in 1989 and replicated on a site near Doe Hall Creek. (Courtesy of Charleston County Public Library.)

Richard Tillia Morrison II (1816–1910), codeveloper of McClellanville, was among the wealthiest St. James Santee planters. He is shown with his second wife, Abigail Morrison. In 1860, he owned over 7,000 acres. The Confederate veteran was a planter, parish magistrate, Wappetaw Independent Church officer, and state legislator. He also pioneered drainage systems to improve his agricultural yield.

Four generations with the same name posed for this family portrait. Seated are Richard Tillia Morrison I and II, father and son, and standing are Richard Tillia Morrison III and IV, grandson and nephew. There is now a Richard Tillia Morrison VII. The first one was born in 1771, so the name has been used for 236 years.

The back of Laurel Hill Plantation indicated a busy household, especially since owner Richard T. Morrison II had 11 children with his first wife, Elizabeth Ann Venning (1817–1859), and 7 more children with his second wife, Eliza Abigail Toomer (1803–1906). The Shakelfords named Laurel Hill when they owned it, and a subsequent owner was a Morrison cousin, Joseph Legare. (Courtesy of Charleston County Public Library.)

103

Tibwin Plantation, established about 1705 with a house built about 1805 four miles south of McClellanville, is the parish's oldest surviving coastal plantation house. William Matthews built Tibwin's first house, and other families followed. In the 1930s, Tibwin's rice mill was purchased for Henry Ford's museum in Michigan. This Tibwin Creek house in Francis Marion National Forest is on the National Register of Historic Places, along with its stable and oak allée. (Courtesy of South Carolina Historical Society.)

Pictured here in 1908, a happy crowd from McClellanville sets off for a picnic at Doe Hall Plantation, five miles south of McClellanville, riding in the village's first mail delivery car. During the Civil War, pickets stationed at Doe Hall prevented Union troop entry. Richard L. Morrison owned the plantation in the early 1900s and lived here before moving to the village. The property remains in his family, but no historic buildings survived.

A palmetto tree marks the head of the Palmetto Trail, an inland hiking path starting at Buck Hall Recreation Area, seven miles south of McClellanville in Francis Marion National Forest. The property was formerly Buck Hall Plantation, owned by Gen. Richard Vanderhorst and later Stephen D. Doar. Its Highway 17 frontage became a freedman's village for African Americans after the Civil War, and ownership continues with their descendants.

Walnut Grove Plantation, nine miles south of McClellanville on Awendaw Creek, retains an avenue of live oaks, stable ruins, and an early 20th-century home no longer used. Salt was produced here during the Civil War. Dr. Horace W. Leland purchased the property after 1875 and grew tobacco and Sea Island cotton. It is now in Francis Marion National Forest.

Walnut Grove Plantation's cemetery is in dense woods near Awendaw Creek. Persons buried there include Alexander Hume Lucas; William Lucas, son of John Hume Lucas; Alice Lucas Rutledge, second wife of Archibald Rutledge; David Doar; Dr. Stephen D. Doar; and two rectors of St. James Santee Episcopal Church, Rev. Nathaniel Hyatt (1846–1865) and Rev. Paul Trapier Prentiss (1910–1913).

Halfway Creek Church, built about 1941, was a ministry of New Wappetaw Presbyterian Church in McClellanville, which was led by Rev. Alva Gregg to assist a nearby rural community in building a church. Now inactive, Halfway Creek chapel in Francis Marion National Forest served the area until its population diminished. In the 19th century, this community had a c. 1828 church.

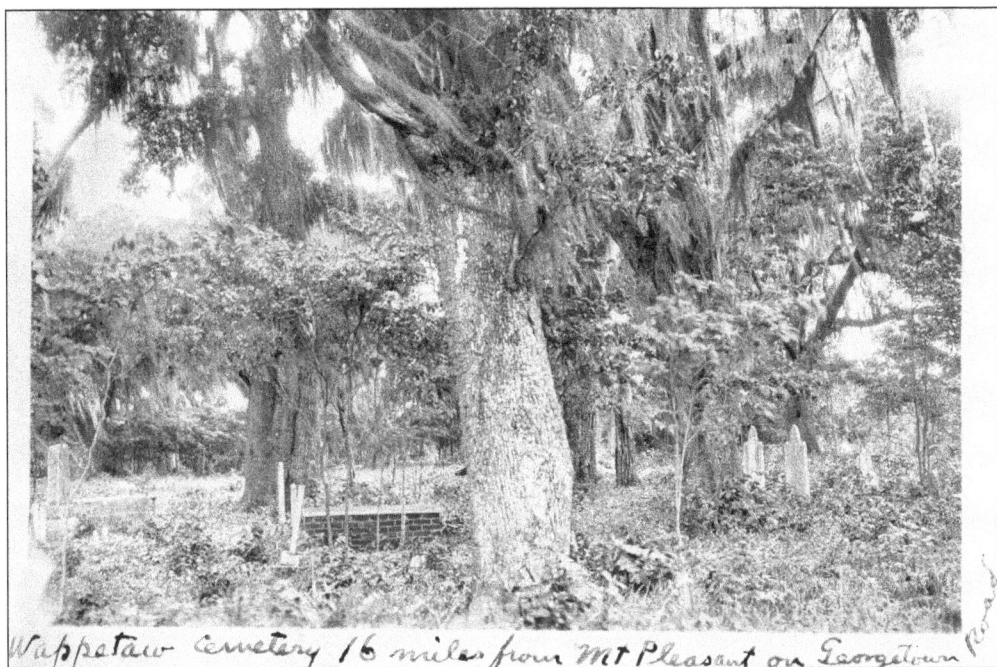

Wappetaw cemetery 16 miles from Mt Pleasant on Georgetown Road

A cemetery is all that remains of Wappetaw Independent Church, also called Old Wappetaw Church, on 15-Mile Landing Road at Seewee Bay. Established about 1696, the original church, a predecessor to New Wappetaw Presbyterian Church in McClellanville, was burned in 1782 by British troops, and its replacement held services until about 1877. It collapsed in decay 20 years later. The cemetery is pictured here about 1930. (Courtesy of South Carolina Historical Society.)

Wren's Methodist Chapel at 1755 Highway 45, also called Moss Swamp Road, was built around 1878 and has a cemetery dating to 1880. It is two miles west of McClellanville on land given by Charles White and was named for builder John J. Wrenn. It replaced the Nazareth Meeting House on Old Kings Highway that burned in the Civil War. The chapel held school classes in the early 1900s and held Catholic church services after 1903, when McClellanville Methodist Church organized.

An 1898 view of the tall light on Lighthouse Island fails to reveal that it leans slightly west because of construction settling. Shown with one of several nearby light-keeper houses, the lighthouse has a cast-iron spiral staircase attached inside its exterior wall. As one climbs the approximately 200 steps, the view improves with each window. Located seven miles east of McClellanville, Lighthouse Island is in Cape Romain National Wildlife Refuge, named by Spanish explorer Lucas de Ayllon, who, in 1524, sailed Carolina's coast seeking a settlement site. Ayllon's San Miguel del Guape, the first European settlement in North America, may be in Winyah Bay near Georgetown or near the Santee River mouth, but it has not been found, despite several archaeological attempts.

Three

OTHER LANDMARKS

Turtle eggs were heavily hunted a century ago, much like wild game and waterfowl. Four unidentified men display a harvest of several hundred eggs, likely taken from a single loggerhead sea turtle nest. The eggs' soft, rubbery shells made them easy to transport, and they reportedly made tastier cakes than poultry eggs. Considered a delicacy, the eggs were hunted for market, endangering the loggerhead species. (Courtesy of Ginny and Michael Prevost.)

Cape parties are a McClellanville tradition; this one took place in the early 1900s. Events ranged from day trips to moonlight cruises to overnight campouts. Participants organized boat transportation to nearby barrier islands, where they held picnics, fried fish, and roasted oysters. They enjoyed fishing, shelling, swimming, singing, seining, crabbing, and courting. Some parties even climbed the lighthouse!

The *Spray* was a passenger and freight boat operating from McClellanville; it also shuttled passengers to Cape parties. It belonged to Capt. Hepburn Morrison and later to Rutledge B. Leland. This view was reportedly captured on April 18, 1908, when a group of villagers arrived at the beach. Other freight and passenger boats supplying McClellanville were the *Carolina*, *Happy Days*, and *Virginia Belle*. (Courtesy of Dr. Walter Bonner.)

Two of four lighthouses built on barrier islands in Cape Romain National Wildlife Refuge remain. The brick structures are in close proximity on Lighthouse Island, previously called Raccoon Key, as was a nearby island that retains that name. The short tower, built about 1827, is 65 feet high. It was replaced after 20 years of deactivation on New Year's Day in 1858 by a 150-foot tower built by slaves and deactivated in 1947. These lights were inactive during the Civil War, from 1861 to 1865. A 1910 view, above, shows multiple buildings in the lighthouse settlement, and an 1893 view, below, shows a light keeper's house between the lights. Furnished housing and a schoolteacher provided by the federal government helped attract lighthouse staff.

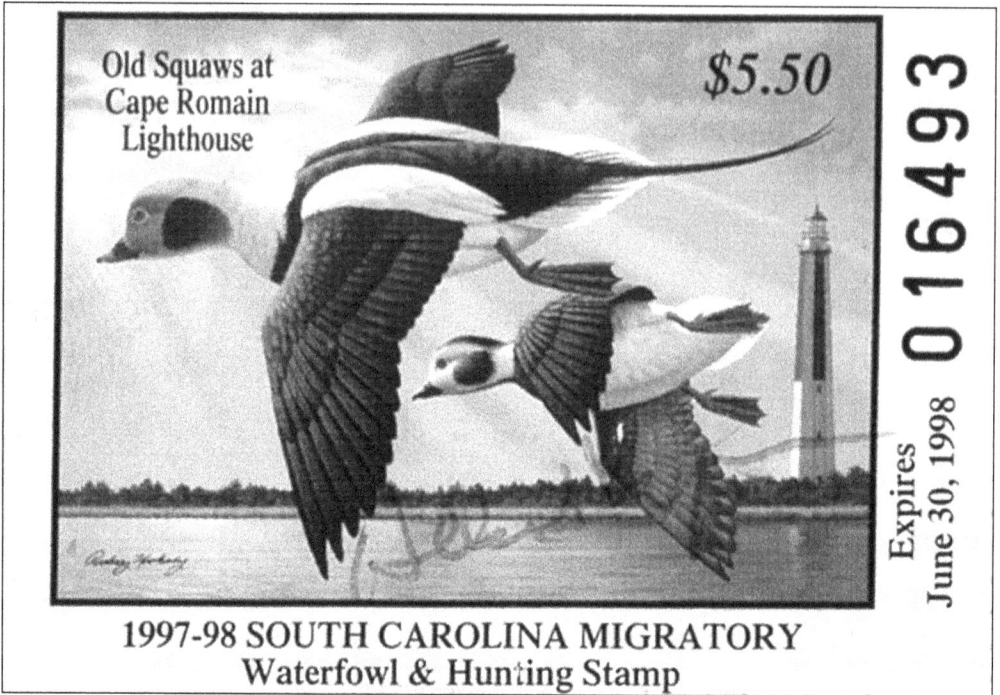

Old Squaws at Cape Romain Lighthouse

$5.50

0 1 6 4 9 3

Expires June 30, 1998

1997-98 SOUTH CAROLINA MIGRATORY
Waterfowl & Hunting Stamp

The 1997–1998 South Carolina Migratory Waterfowl and Hunting stamp, shown enlarged, featured ducks flying past Lighthouse Island's tall light. The wildlife refuge, established in 1932, is an ideal shore-bird rookery. Its original parcels were purchased for $2.84 per acre, and it now has 65,000 acres, managed by the U.S. Fish and Wildlife Service and encompassing 22 miles of coastal South Carolina. (Courtesy of Jim Grayson.)

August Frederick Wichmann (1868–1956), lighthouse keeper from 1913 to 1934, and Ruth Wichmann, his third wife, lived in the government-furnished cottage by Lighthouse Island's tall light. The second-longest tenured keeper was the light's first keeper, Thadeus C. Skrine, who served from 1839 to 1857. Social isolation led to the departure of most keepers and assistants within a few years.

Swimmers are pictured in the early 1900s on Jeremy Island, recently added to Cape Romain National Wildlife Refuge. A rudimentary island clubhouse made it a popular beach for villagers. The two-mile-long island was bisected by the Intracoastal Waterway, and 1,018 acres remain, mostly marsh lands. It belonged to the McClellans in the 19th century and to the DuPres of Palmetto Plantation in the 20th century.

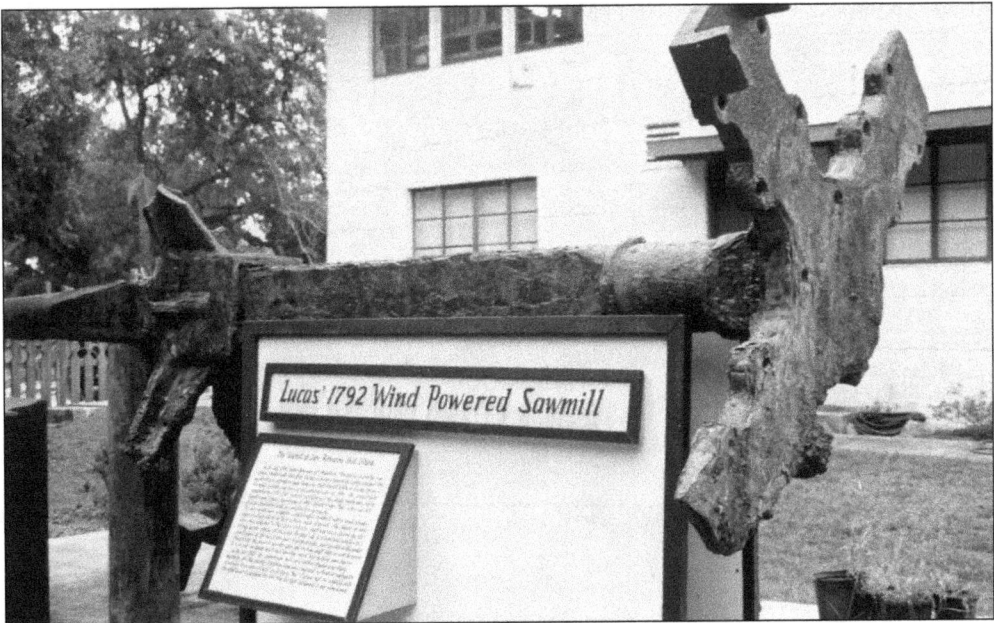

Part of the 24-foot driveshaft from the wind-powered Mill Island sawmill, designed in 1792 by Jonathan Lucas, is displayed at the Village Museum in McClellanville. The mill was on a remote marsh island behind Lighthouse Island, both now part of the wildlife refuge. Lucas earlier pioneered the steam-driven rice mill. Prominent display of his machinery attests to its dynamic impact on St. James, Santee Parish and other rice regions.

Bulls Island guesthouse, shown here about 1941, was a former residence of Gayer G. Dominick, who transferred the island to the federal government in 1936, after maintaining it for 11 years as a hunting retreat. There are remnants of an 18th-century tower or fort on this island, which saw activity in the Revolutionary and Civil Wars. The 5,000-acre Bulls Island has over 337 bird species and is accessible by ferry from Moore's Landing in Awendaw.

On March 18, 1865, *Harper's Weekly* depicted the "Landing of Gen. Potter's and Adm. Dahlgren's ships at Bull's Bay." Ironically, by then Dahlgren's *Harvest Moon* lay submerged in Winyah Bay near Georgetown, a one-time victory in which the Confederacy sank an admiral's flagship, and it remains there. This amphibious landing made up the Union's effort to draw Confederate forces from Charleston so Gen. William T. Sherman could burn the city; instead he burned Columbia.

From 1852 to 1897, Bulls Bay lighthouse was a tower extension of the light keeper's residence. Only 35 feet high, it was built at the northeast point of the island's six-mile expanse and survived 45 years before the Atlantic Ocean claimed it during a storm. A metal-frame lighthouse, erected in 1900, was deactivated in 1913 and dismantled. Marine navigational advances eliminated the need for lighthouses, but they remain popular nostalgic symbols.

The Seewee shell ring in Francis Marion National Forest in Awendaw was 150 feet in diameter until it was cut through by the Intracoastal Waterway in the 1930s. This is an aerial view of an intact shell ring nearby. The circular coastal deposits of oyster shells contain Native American pottery shards, animal bones, teeth, and pieces of antler. These rare 3,500-year-old midden rings are unique to the Southeast, but their significance is unknown.

Shellmore Oyster Produce Company, shown in the 1930s, was an oyster cannery located on a salt marsh five and a half miles south of McClellanville. The company had another cannery on Jeremy Creek that also canned vegetables. It normally employed about 200 workers, with additional workers added during harvest season. A residential community retains the name and locale of the original cannery, which operated during the first half of the 20th century. (Courtesy of Debbie Thames Hattaway.)

The 32-Mile House, or Jones Tavern, was a pre-Revolutionary stagecoach tavern on Old Kings Highway at the junction of five roads. It was 32 miles from Charleston and once run by Elias Jones. Entry steps are the visible remains of the tavern, razed in the 1950s but shown here c. 1930. Nearby were a highway section used as a horseracing track; Straight Reach; and Nazareth Meeting House, the parish's earliest Methodist church, which later burned. (Courtesy of South Carolina Historical Society.)

Old Kings Highway, or Old Georgetown Road, began as a Native American path and became a stagecoach road with tavern inns at intervals, which provided accommodations for travelers and their horses. Luther Jones, left, and Alec Jones, right, are shown here in a horse-drawn wagon on an unpaved highway section in Francis Marion National Forest. Alec Jones ran the Jones Ferry at the South Santee River. (Courtesy of Sarah Nell Scott.)

Round brick towers were built as slave hurricane shelters in the Santee Delta after an 1822 hurricane drowned nearly 300 slaves. A restored tower is pictured here. The emancipation of slaves in 1865, followed by hurricanes in 1893 and 1916, shaped parish history, as planter families moved their permanent residency to McClellanville for economic and social gain.

Santee Gun Club house, built about 1905 at 220 Santee Gun Club Road on the former Blake's Plantation adjoining the South Santee River, was also called Blake House. Twelve South Santee River rice plantations consolidated to form the gun club's 25,000 acres. Now managed by the South Carolina Department of Natural Resources, it is Santee Coastal Reserve Wildlife Management Area, containing the Nature Conservancy's Washo Reserve, an egret and ibis rookery.

A hunter proudly displays doves draped over a car at the Santee Gun Club. Formed by wealthy New Yorkers and Philadelphians, the club was renowned as one of America's finest waterfowl-hunting retreats. Membership was limited to 30 individuals, and the cumulative membership roster was an honor roll of American capitalists. Pres. Grover Cleveland hunted with Santee Gun Club.

An unidentified African American youth balances a basket on his head at Santee Gun Club in the early 20th century. The club increased its duck population by employing nearby African American laborers to cultivate rice in designated shooting fields. These employees descended from Santee River plantation slaves.

Francis Marion National Forest is a 250,000-acre forest managed to preserve natural resources and named for the "Swamp Fox," Gen. Francis Marion (1732–1795). He excelled at guerilla warfare in the Revolutionary War, hiding his volunteer army in Lowcountry swamps, disabling British supply lines, and eluding retribution by moving constantly. A U.S. Forest Service office at 1015 Pinckney Street in McClellanville manages the forest.

This is the strategic view of the South Santee River from Battery Warren, built in 1862. It is an L-shaped Confederate earthen embankment, likely constructed by slaves and occupied by Confederate guns from December 1862 to November 1864. The fort was on the riverfront of Col. Samuel Warren's South Santee River plantation, Echaw Grove. Designed to prevent Union troops from advancing upriver, the fort in Francis Marion National Forest was 20 feet high.

C. T. 14—The Tomb of Francis Marion, Famous Revolutionary General

A 1944 postcard shows Francis Marion's tomb at Belle Isle Plantation, home of his brother, Gabriel Marion, in Berkeley County near the Frances Marion National Forest. Marion was born on a Winyah Bay plantation later renamed Belle Isle. The forest named for him sustained major damage in Hurricane Hugo, including the loss of most loblolly and longleaf pine trees over nine inches in diameter. Recovery will take about 100 years.

120

A rocky South Santee River bluff was chosen by French Huguenots in 1685 as the site of their settlement, Jamestown. The area was named French Santee for the immigrant families who farmed it. English settlers located nearby, creating a total population of several hundred families. However, flooding and extended isolation discouraged the settlers, who abandoned their town and surrounding area in the 18th century. (Courtesy of South Carolina Historical Society.)

About 1930, an African American man pointed out the remains of the Jamestown Church in the French Santee town. The land became part of Mount Moriah Plantation, which belonged to Col. Samuel Jerman Palmer (1807–1853), whose holdings once exceeded 18,500 acres and 200 slaves. He also owned land opposite McClellanville on Jeremy Creek, which he called "The Seashore," as well as Gravel Hill, Pinetree, and Polebridge Plantations. (Courtesy of South Carolina Historical Society.)

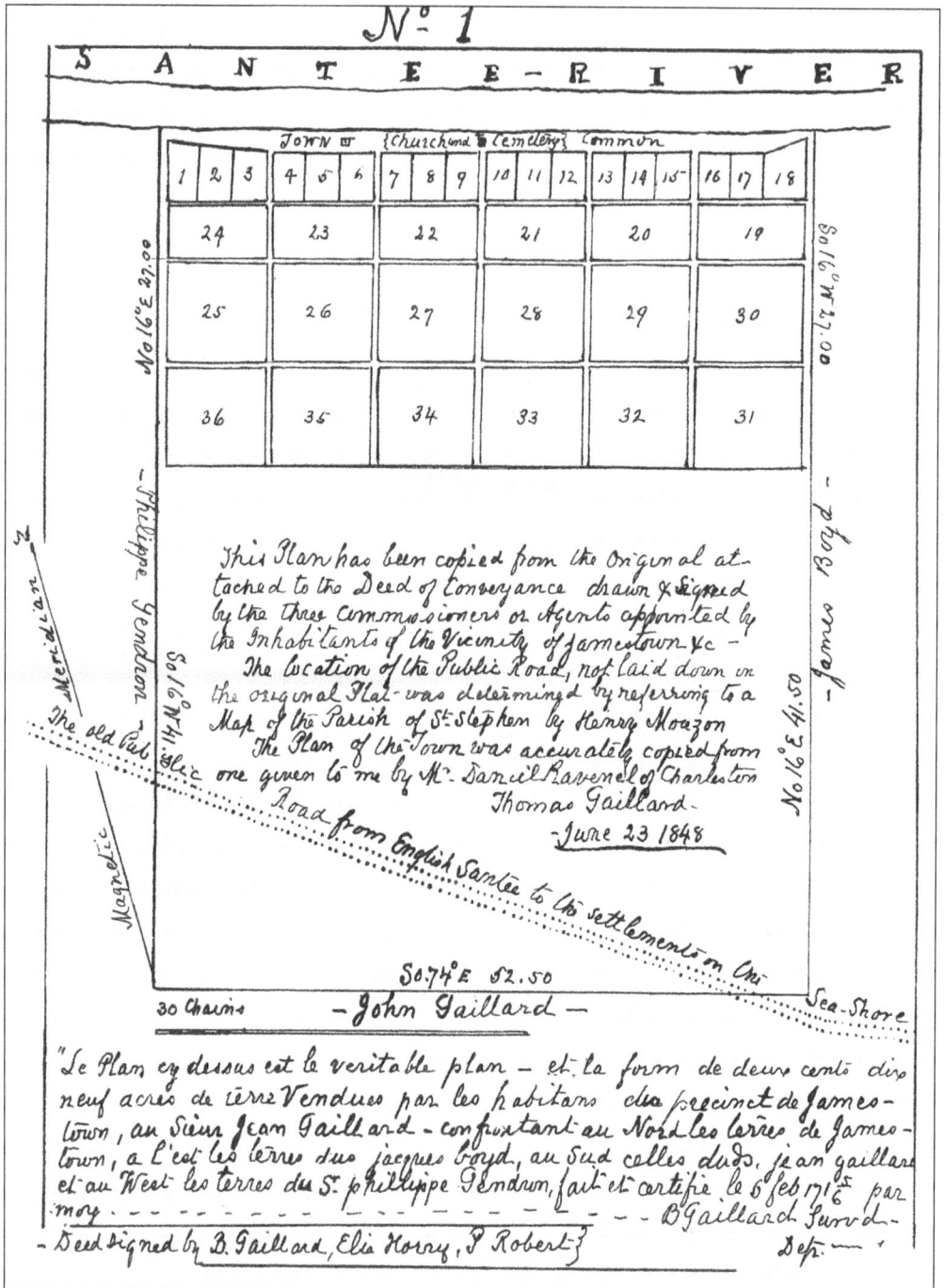

An 1848 copy of the 1716 map of Jamestown reveals an orderly South Santee River village of 31 lots, which decrease in size as they approach the town commons, a long, narrow band of river frontage reserved for a church and cemetery. A river road leading to the coast passed through the lower, undivided portion of this 1685 settlement. After this village was abandoned, Jamestown's name was later affixed to a new town established upriver on higher land. Natural limestone deposits in the early settlement's vicinity are now being mined.

Wappetaw Bridge crossed Wappetaw Creek on 15-Mile Landing Road, near the former site of Wappetaw Independent Church. Pictured around 1930, the wooden bridge was near a Colonial tavern, 15-Mile House, and a camp frequently used by Francis Marion during the Revolution. A large oak tree nearby was named the Cornwallis Oak, and British generals Cornwallis and Tarleton had encampments here. (Courtesy of South Carolina Historical Society.)

A memorable freeze on December 31, 1917, resulted in ice four inches thick on the surface of the Santee River. Here an unidentified African American man stands on the ice beside a small boat at an unspecified river location. Other views of this rare freeze include the Santee Gun Club's boat, *Happy Days*, gridlocked in ice. (Courtesy of Ginny and Michael Prevost.)

Santee Hotel, Ferguson, S. C.

The Santee Hotel, shown on this 1912 postcard, and the town of Ferguson were permanently flooded when Santee Cooper formed Lake Marion by damming the Santee River to create hydroelectric power around 1940. Reduced output from the Santee River system increased the river's salinity and decreased alluvial nutrients for saltwater marine life, both of which negatively impacted regional ecology and fishing industries.

A Moonshine Still

Hell Hole Swamp near Jamestown was infamous for illicit moonshine and related lawlessness in the 1930s, when a Lowcountry backwoods still was exposed. Mason jars in the foreground, left, were standard receptacles for "white lightning," or corn whiskey, which was highly profitable and easy to produce. The heyday of bootleg whiskey was during Prohibition, from 1920 to 1933.

124

FREEMAN'S COTTAGES

On Ocean Highway

U.S. 17

AWENDAW

SOUTH, CAROLINA

Freeman's Cottages on Highway 17 one mile north of Awendaw Creek was a 1940s tourist motel with a dining room on the premises. This advertising postcard targeted hunters and fishermen, who likely provided most of the motel's business. Only the two-story building remains; it became a gas station and is now a residence with a brick-veneer exterior.

Awendaw Bridge is picturesque + for generations it has been suggested that its headwaters be dredged to those of Wando to improve the inland coastal waterway systems.

Awendaw Creek Bridge was a wooden span in the 1930s, when traffic was infrequent and automobiles weren't nearly as heavy as modern vehicles. A concrete bridge replaced the wooden one, but the marsh-bordered creek that forms the southern coastal boundary of St. James, Santee Parish remains a scenic location on Highway 17. (Courtesy of South Carolina Historical Society.)

Edgewater Motel and Restaurant, shown here about 1950, was on Highway 17 at Awendaw Creek, opposite St. James, Santee Parish. Owned by B. H. Thames, it had a McClellanville telephone number and included a restaurant that was open from 7:00 a.m. to midnight. After the motel closed, its buildings became a garment factory.

The South Santee River Ferry landing on Old Kings Highway was the starting point of a journey to Georgetown that involved ferry crossings of the South Santee, North Santee, and Sampit Rivers. Bridges replaced all three ferries by 1928. Here Dot Beckman of McClellanville, center, and her unidentified companions begin the journey.

126

Aerial View of Cooper River Bridge—Ocean Highway U. S. 17
Between Charleston and Georgetown, S. C.

The 1929 opening of Grace Memorial Bridge over the Cooper River, like the Santee River bridge openings, was heralded as imminent economic prosperity for McClellanville, a remote extremity in Charleston County. However, results were that residents increasingly shopped out of town, and local businesses declined. Shown here in the 1940s, the Cooper River span cost about $6 million.

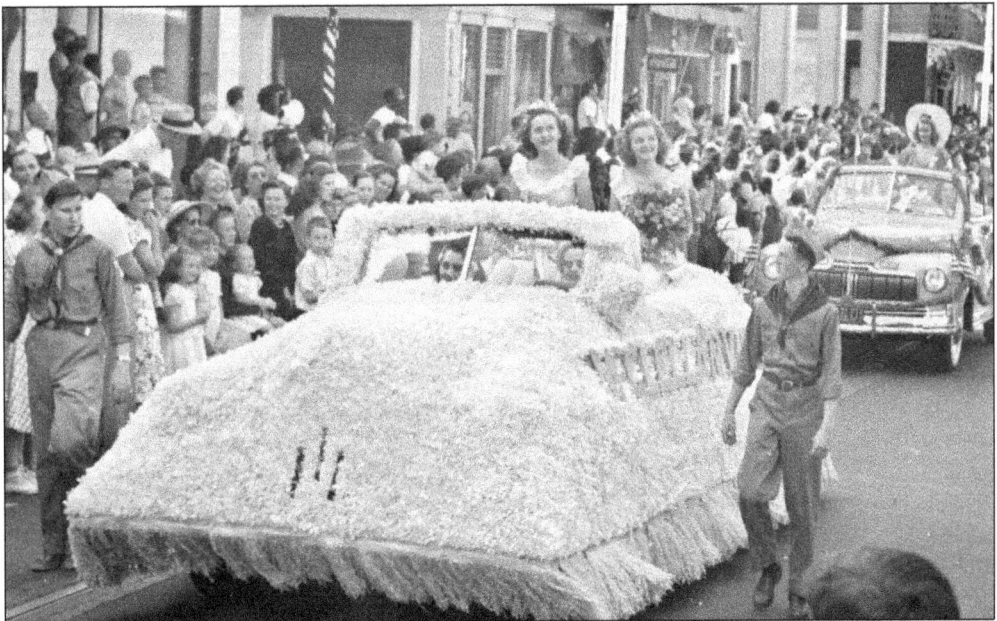

Village beauties Betty Ward (left) and Phillis Barrett rode a McClellanville parade float in a c. 1950 Azalea Festival parade on King Street in Charleston. The annual event celebrated flowering azalea plants. Blooms ranging from white to shades of pink, red, coral, and lavender abound in the Lowcountry, forming stunning displays of natural beauty.

Visit us at
arcadiapublishing.com